EUROPA ✠ MILITARIA
SPECIAL N°7

WORLD WAR II
BRITISH WOMEN'S UNIFORMS

IN COLOUR PHOTOGRAPHS

MARTIN BRAYLEY
& RICHARD INGRAM

Windrow & Greene

©Martin Brayley & Richard Ingram

Designed by John Anastasio/Creative Line
Printed in Spain

This edition published
in Great Britain 1995 by
Windrow & Greene Ltd.
5 Gerrard Street
London W1V 7LJ

A CIP catalogue record for this book is available from the
British Library.

ISBN 1 85915 032 2

Acknowledgements:

Many people have given freely of their time and knowledge
during the preparation of this book, and without their help
many sections would have been incomplete. Some have lent
a single item of kit, others have given free access to their
collections; the models have spent many hours in the studio
dressed in somewhat unfamiliar attire. The authors wish to
express their gratitude to all the individuals and institutions
who have helped with and encouraged this project,
including, in alphabetical order: Mike Barnes, Lynette
Brayley, Louise Baverstock, Dee Beresford, Madelaine
Browne, Alwyn Bryant of the Royal Armouries, Angie
Burke, Fiona Campbell, Isabelle Campion, Captain
J.Cotterell QARANC, Teresa Davies, Aileen Derrit, Russell
Docherty, Deborah Draper, Zoe Elizabeth, Tom & Jackie
Gates, Pat Gould, Nick Hall of Sabre Sales, Barry Hardy,
Gary Hancock, Phil Haycock, George Hazel of Tangmere
Aviation Museum, Annie Keir, Rachel King, the Trustees of
the Imperial War Museum, Major (Retd.) M.H.McCombe of
the QARANC Museum, Stuart McKenzie of Brooklands
Military Society, Portsmouth City Museum, Tony and Joan
Poucher, Emma Roberts, Emma Robinson, Royal Military
Police Museum Chichester, Michelle Small, Robert
Stedman, Marie Taylor, Penny Taylor, Lesley Thomas of the
Royal Naval Museum, Melanie Ward, Suzie Whitehouse,
Tony Wood of Ego Hairdressers, Karen Woolger, and Liz
Valentine.

Dedications:

To all of the "Women in Uniform" 1939-1945 - they also
served.
And to the memory of PO(AEA) Mark Brayley,
815 Naval Air Squadron (1969-1994)

CONTENTS

INTRODUCTION

At their peak strengths during World War II the women's services of the British armed forces numbered only slightly short of half a million. They served in a total of some 300 "trades", the great majority of them freeing men for active combat service. From the predictably conservative range of largely clerical rear area duties envisaged by the authorities at the outbreak of war, the roles played by women of all ranks soon expanded enormously, and included service under fire on operational airfields and anti-aircraft gun sites and in overseas combat zones. Death and wounds were no respecters of gender.

The ever-growing band of collectors and historians specialising in women's uniforms have waited for many years for a "dedicated" reference book. Many books on the women's services have been published since the end of World War II, the majority of them general historical studies, or accounts of an individual's service. While they are all valuable references

for collectors and historians, few show evidence of any effort to describe or illustrate in detail the uniforms and equipment worn. Women's uniforms have been included, usually fairly briefly, in general studies; but have long deserved their own volume.

This book is by no means definitive, but it does cover the majority of uniform types worn by the three women's military services. (We are aware of the demand for comparable reference on the uniformed civilian services, but for obvious reasons of space these have been omitted, regretfully, from the present book.) No apologies are made for the imbalance of this book in its inevitable bias towards the Auxiliary Territorial Service: the ATS had by far the greatest variety of uniforms and utility variations. The WRNS had a very limited issue of uniform items and were hardly affected by utility measures; and both the WRNS and to a lesser degree the WAAF tended to rely on available smaller sized male clothing for many trades, such as boat crews and mechanics.

All the uniforms and ephemera illustrated are from the period 1938 to 1945, the majority forming part of the authors' combined collections. We have tried to illustrate a fair proportion of makers' labels for the assistance of collectors in identifying and authenticating these garments.

The authors are currently researching the uniforms of the WLA, AFS, and other civilian services, and those of the Allied nations of the period 1939 to 1945.

THE WOMEN'S ROYAL NAVAL SERVICE

The female auxiliaries of the Senior Service were to provide support to a service whose wartime role was central to the preservation of Britain and her Empire. Without the Royal Navy guarding our shores from the early threat of invasion, and patrolling the sea lanes by which the vital convoys sustained our ability to fight on, the nation would not have survived the onslaught of Nazi Germany. When opportunities arose to take the fight to the enemy it was the Royal Navy which took the initiative, playing a leading role in every theatre of operations. Throughout the long years of war the WRNS played a vital part in Britain's naval effort. Not only did they release countless men for sea service; many trades were manned almost entirely by "Wrens".

The WRNS was formed early in 1939. Influenced by memories of the women's service in World War I, the Admiralty had initially envisaged only the part-time use of small numbers of locally recruited volunteers drawn mainly from the relatives of serving and former naval personnel. At first their trades were limited mainly to "domestic" employment, writers, and packers, with a few officers in cypher training; the most dynamic duty at that time fell to the motor transport driver, who was expected to have a limited knowledge of the vehicle in her charge. The first officers' training course took place late in 1939, with the WRNS rating course starting in January 1940, although for some months before this untrained personnel were at work in their domestic trades.

During 1941-42 the urgent need to release fit men for sea service brought about the rapid expansion of the WRNS, not only in numbers employed but also in diversity of trades. More than 100,000 women would serve during the war, in some 90 rating and 50 officer categories, with a peak strength of 74,620 in September 1944. The men of the Royal Navy were soon to recognise and respect the competence and cheerfulness with which Wrens set about any task presented to them. Many Allied convoys were hardly in sight of land when, regardless of the weather, they were met by a WRNS boarding officer: "It's a woman!" became a familiar exclamation. Upon setting sail once more it was invariably a Wren who went to sea to hand over the sailing orders, and the sight of her undoubtedly brightened the day of departure for many a sailor.

The WRNS served the Royal Navy at home and across the globe, from the largest naval establishment to the smallest and most remote Nissen hut outpost. Few actually served afloat (though some did, as cypher officers and coder ratings aboard large transports); but otherwise they undertook work in all trades, both those accepted half a century ago as being "women's work" and many which had previously been the jealously guarded domain of men. (Despite orders that women should not be engaged in the firing of weapons, WRNS gun teams are known to have manned twin Lewis gun AA mountings on remote naval air stations.)

WRNS UNIFORM

The Admiralty, like the War Office and Air Ministry, had perceived only limited roles for the women who were to free men for the fleet. Writer, driver, cook, steward or storekeeper were typical of the tasks envisaged. Typical of all the women's services, too, would be the initial shortage of uniforms with which to equip the surge of willing volunteers in 1939/40. For many the only item issued for months was a brassard bearing the letters "WRNS" for wear on the sleeve of civilian clothing.

In time a coarse navy blue serge uniform was issued, inspired by that worn during World War I but adapted to some extent to match the currently fashionable civilian style. It consisted of a double-breasted jacket with two internal skirt pockets with external rectangular flaps, a skirt cut to just below the knee, and for junior ranks a soft-crowned, floppy-brimmed gabardine hat. Beneath the tunic a white detachable-collar shirt was worn with a black tie. Black lisle stockings and plain black leather shoes finished off the uniform. Initially only one suit was issued, but by 1943/44 most Wrens possessed an extra "best" uniform.

(Left) This Wren is wearing the post-1942 style of cap. It bears the traditional Royal Navy cap tally, in this case the wartime "HMS" introduced as a security measure; however, it was not uncommon to see establishment and occasionally even ships' names being worn. The double-breasted tunic fastens on the left side with a double row of black horn buttons bearing the naval crown and fouled anchor. On the right sleeve note the "Steward" trade badge; all WRNS rank and trade badges were embroidered in light blue.

(Below) A WRNS W/T operator - note her trade badge - undergoing Morse training with a visual signalling lamp. She is wearing the pre-August 1942 soft gabardine hat.

(Below) Detail of the WRNS black lisle stockings, this pair dated 1944 and made by R.R.& C. under the brand name "Canasta." Finer quality rayon stockings were also worn by Wrens when they could be obtained.

(Right) WRNS Petty Officer. The uniform is basically that issued to junior rates but with the addition of gilt buttons to the tunic front, two small ornamental buttons on each cuff, and the Petty Officers' rank badge. CPO Wrens would have worn three full size buttons along the lower cuff, and small blue trade badges on the collar fronts. Cap badges were a blue thread version of those worn by male senior rates, worn on the WRNS officer-style tricorn hat (see page 13).

(Left) A group of WRNS ratings, senior rates, and a Second Officer photographed at a naval air station in 1945.

7

WRNS BOAT CREW

The first Wrens to enter this trade began their training in 1941. They were to serve on small craft such as tugboats and harbour launches, which in many cases were manned entirely by Wrens. When qualified they were required to have a good knowledge of seamanship, navigation and signalling, complemented by the physical stamina required to perform their arduous duties effectively.

The standard WRNS uniform was impractical for boat crews, and as there was no woman's alternative small sizes of men's square-neck vests ("white fronts") and bell-bottom trousers were issued. These were worn with the WRNS tunic, and white plimsolls - necessary to provide a sure footing on the boat decks - worn with or without socks. Boat crews were allowed the distinction of wearing a white lanyard, in male rating's fashion, under the collar of the tunic when wearing boating dress. The seaman's knife was also issued.

For extra warmth in colder weather WRNS boat crews (along with other essentially outdoor working trades such as MT drivers) were issued heavy woollen stockings and blue woollen drawers. "Loan" clothing included two-piece coverall suits, watch coats, duffle coats, oilskins, and sea boots.

(Left) This Wren is wearing her "boat crew rig" comprising small sizes of the man's pattern square-necked cotton "white front", serge trousers (bell-bottoms), and white plimsolls with black rubber soles. Note the front flap opening of the trousers.

(Below) Boat crew rig worn complete with the standard WRNS double-breasted tunic. Note the white lanyard worn around the neck, as it would be by male ratings in "square rig"; this was a jealously guarded privilege extended only to boat crew and boom defence Wrens.

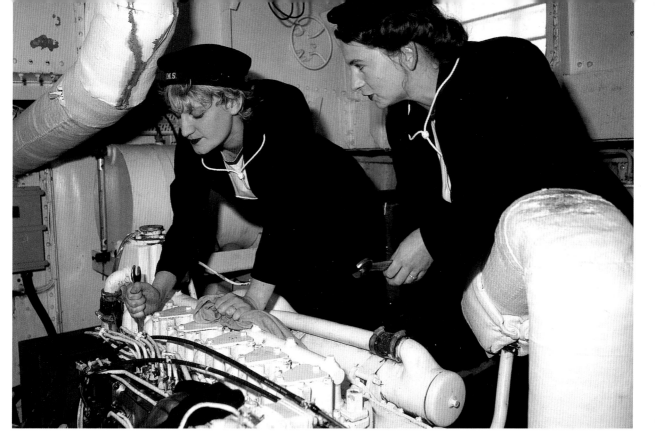

(**Above**) Two boat crew Wrens conducting running repairs in the engine room of their harbour launch, one of the many skills mastered by this WRNS category.

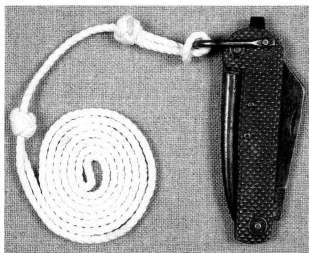

(**Left**) The issue seaman's clasp knife attached to its white lanyard. The knife has a cutting blade and a marlin spike, essential for splicing and general ropework. The knife was normally worn on its lanyard and carried around the waist.

(**Below**) WRNS "housewife" and contents. This small kit included the items necessary to keep the uniform in good repair; note underwear elastic, lisle darning thread, and WRNS-marked needles.

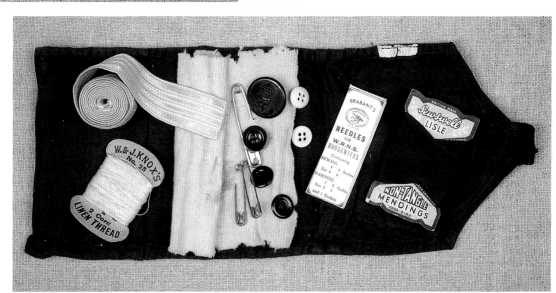

WRNS RATING'S GREATCOAT

As early as the beginning of 1940 the Admiralty, ahead of the other services, had realised the need for the issue of a heavyweight overcoat for its women auxiliaries. When introduced the issue greatcoat for the WRNS bore a strong resemblance to that of male naval personnel. Prior to its issue WRNS had made do with a gabardine raincoat; initially procured from civilian retailers, it was adequate for wet weather but not particularly warm.

In keeping with tradition the WRNS greatcoat was of the double-breasted "lancer" style, fastening to the left with a double row of four black horn (later plastic) buttons bearing the naval crown and anchor. Just below waist level on each side there was a flap-topped slash pocket. The rear of the coat was plain with the exception of a pleat running from shoulder to waist level, and a lower vent running from just below the waist to the bottom of the skirt, closed by buttons; there was no half-belt. Internally the body was three-quarter lined and the sleeves fully lined with a black cotton sateen fabric.

A similar style of coat, the "watchcoat", was issued as a loan clothing item to those requiring a warm work coat. This bore a strong resemblance to the greatcoat but was single-breasted and designed to be worn long, coming nearly to the ankles. ("Loan" clothing items were those held in a common clothing store, issued to individuals when their duties required them and subsequently returned.)

(Left) A Wren rating wearing the issue greatcoat over her uniform. As prescribed by the military authorities, the respirator is being "carried at all times".

(Below) WRNS shoes. Of plain black leather, they have a double row of four eyelets, with leather soles and heels. This pair were manufactured by Gidley Wright in 1945.

(**Above left**) The service respirator, with its haversack - khaki for all three armed services - and contents. These include Mk VI anti-dim ointment, ointment anti-gas No.2, anti-gas eyeshields Mk II, cotton waste for use in blotting liquid vesicants; and, here, a pair of issue respirator spectacles - sturdy prescription spectacles provided for those who needed them, in sprung frames which could be worn under the respirator.

(**Above**) Detail of the respirator haversack, which has been personalised by the addition of a WRNS crest - a naval crown laid over an anchor and surmounted by a wren.

(**Left**) Detail from a photograph of Wrens having lunch aboard a visiting US warship. The Wrens seated at the front are wearing the dark blue gabardine raincoat, which since the beginning of the war had been listed on the scale of issue for WRNS ratings. (Imperial War Museum)

WRNS OFFICER'S SERVICE DRESS

Following the practice of the other two women's services, the WRNS officer's uniform was based on that worn by male officers of the Royal Navy. The double-breasted tunic was made of a fine quality navy blue barathea, diagonal serge or "doe skin", with two slash pockets at the skirt and a small slash pocket on the left breast (a small white decorative handkerchief was often carried in this pocket.) It was secured by a double row of four gilt buttons bearing the naval crown and fouled anchor design with a rope surround. Light blue rank lacing was worn at each cuff; the upper lace for all ranks was surmounted by a diamond rather than by the circle used in male officers' rank lace. Unlike the ATS and WAAF the WRNS opted for a tunic buttoning on the ladies' side; and for a skirt of comparatively attractive cut with a double box pleat. This uniform was undoubtedly the most pleasing of those worn by the women's services.

WRNS rank structure

WRNS Officer's Rank	Royal Navy Equivalent
Chief Commandant	Rear Admiral
Commandant	Commodore
Superintendent	Captain
Chief Officer	Commander
First Officer	Lieutenant Commander
Second Officer	Lieutenant
Third Officer	Sub Lieutenant

(Left & below) A WRNS Second Officer, her rank identified by the two blue rings on each cuff. This officer is wearing the uniform adopted at the time the WRNS were formed, and which remained unchanged throughout the war. Note the smart double box pleats in the skirt, the tunic buttoned on the ladies' side (i.e. right over left) with a double row of four buttons, and light blue rank lacing and diamond at the cuff.

(Left) The WRNS tricorn hat worn by officers and senior rates. The WRNS officer's cap badge has a light blue wreath surrounding the fouled anchor device, in place of the gold wreath of the otherwise identical man's pattern.

(Below) WRNS identity disc belonging to First Officer M.James. This crudely stamped disc was probably used to identify the owner of a respirator or steel helmet rather than being worn by the officer.

(Below) The WRNS officer's greatcoat, worn here by a group chatting with a Fleet Air Arm pilot. A smart and functional garment that was also very warm, it was secured with a double row of six gilt buttons, and bore shoulder boards displaying rank.

WRNS OVERALLS & WORKWEAR

Introduced into the Royal Navy in the late 1930s as men's workwear, the one-piece combination suit was also issued to Wrens. It was categorised as loan clothing, and was first issued (on a scale of one suit per rating) to WRNS MT drivers in 1940. As the war progressed and the number of WRNS trades increased they were issued to all trades who needed them for their work; these included all mechanics, qualified ordnance personnel, and torpedo Wrens. The scale of issue was also increased to two suits per rating.

The overall was a very simple garment, manufactured in heavy duty dark blue cotton twill which faded rapidly with repeated washing and wear. Although generally similar two types of overall existed, the earlier having a fly front fastening and the later version exposed buttons. Both had a small buttoned pocket on the left breast and an adjustable half-belt at the rear waist.

(Left) A WRNS rating (Qualified Ordnance) wearing the fly-fronted version of the one-piece working overall. She wears the man's square-necked "white front" underneath rather than the dark blue work shirt and tie. She is working on a 20mm Oerlikon cannon, and carries that weapon's heavy drum magazine. Many Wrens were employed in the maintenance of the weapons used on Coastal Forces craft and at Combined Operations bases. In an effort to draw in this shapeless garment this Wren has buckled a naval issue "money belt" around her waist. She wears her cap, although it was not unknown for Wrens to wear a black beret for such duties.

(Right) A second type of workwear was also issued to Wrens; this was a simple two-piece cotton twill suit designed for male ratings. The jacket was mid-thigh length, with an open-top pocket below the waist at each side; the trousers were of the "bib and brace" style. It is being worn here by a Wren Battery Charger, a small trade group amalgamated with Maintenance (Air) in late 1942. (Imperial War Museum)

(Below) The WRNS ratings' sailor-type cap introduced in mid-1942. Inspired by the male ratings' cap, it differed mainly in having a soft, unstiffened crown. This example bears the standard wartime "HMS" tally.

(Right) This Wren, working on the engine of a Motor Torpedo Boat, is wearing men's overalls, and the dark blue headscarf (characteristic of wartime civilian fashion) designed to keep the hair clean and safely tucked away while working with machinery. (Imperial War Museum)

(Below right) The issue white shirt with its starched collar was not worn while undertaking dirty work other than domestic chores. For mechanics and others a dark blue/black workshirt with separate collar was issued; this was more comfortable, and did not show oil and dirt stains so readily. Although she has not got a particularly dirty job this Cine Operator has opted to wear the blue shirt.

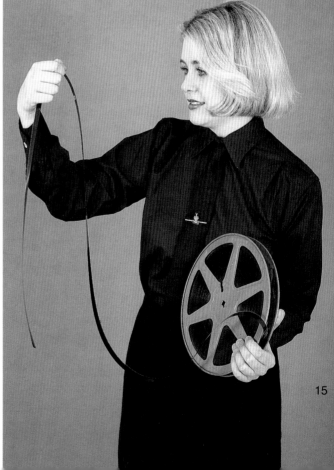

15

WRNS WORKING DRESS

As early as 1940 the Admiralty had developed coveralls for use by WRNS stewards and cooks - two of the earlier roles then believed suitable for the Navy's women auxiliaries. The blue and white pinstriped cooks' coverall was a knee-length garment with a full-length buttoned front closure, short sleeves, and a patch pocket on either thigh. The collar, pockets and sleeves had a wide blue edge trim. These coveralls were also worn by laundry maids and cleaners. Cooks would also wear a white cotton apron and a chef's hat or headscarf.

Officers' stewards had a white knee-length coverall with a full-length fly front; the stand-up collar and cuffs were trimmed with blue.

New entry Wrens undergoing preliminary training had to serve fourteen days before receiving a full issue of kit. In the meantime they were issued as loan clothing a blue lancer-front workdress secured by a double row of four buttons.

By 1944 a simple short-sleeved navy blue cotton twill dress had been introduced for wear by Wrens requiring a working coverall and those undergoing training. This had a half-length front closure secured by four plastic buttons; two open-top thigh pockets fastened by buttons; and a buttoned waist belt.

(**Left**) This Wren is wearing the white coverall issued to officers' stewards; note its blue-trimmed collar and cuffs. It is worn here with the blue fabric money belt; white gloves would also be worn with this dress when necessary.

(**Below**) A Cecil Beaton study of a WRNS cook. She is wearing the blue and white pinstriped cooks' coverall trimmed with blue, with a white apron and and chef's hat, and is surrounded by the tools of her trade. (Imperial War Museum)

(**Right**) The late war blue working dress; note the buttoned belt and thigh pockets. This dress is being worn without a shirt and tie. The label in this example is marked "Harrods 1944 Tropical"; typical of naval labelling, it gives little detail, and despite the tropical reference this dress was certainly issued as general workwear.

(**Below**) The lancer-front dark blue dress issued to Wrens at the Provisional Training School. This fine Cecil Beaton study shows the double row of buttons on the front. (Imperial War Museum)

WRNS TROPICAL UNIFORM

At the beginning of 1941 a carefully selected group of twenty volunteer CPO Wrens and one Second Officer were to be the first Wrens drafted to a foreign shore. Their new station was to be Singapore, which meant that an issue of tropical clothing was required. This took the form of a white short-sleeved dress secured at the front from collar to waist with a row of five brass buttons (later versions would have only four.) It had an open-top patch pocket on either thigh, and a buckleless waistbelt fastened with hooks and eyes. Interestingly, women's tropical clothing was not listed by the Admiralty until September 1941, some months after its first issue. Accessories issued at this time included white hat covers (for the first pattern hat), white lisle stockings and white canvas shoes.

By 1942 a two-piece pattern of tropical uniform had appeared, having a white cotton blouse of more feminine cut, with shoulder darts. The white skirt was plain by comparison. With the introduction of the new style cap in 1942 a tropical version was introduced; identical in style to the new blue pattern, it had a white cotton crown. White cotton ankle socks were frequently worn in preference to white stockings.

(**Above**) This photograph shows the tropical dress with four-button front being worn by a Chief Petty Officer Wren W/T Operator (note trade badges on collar). She is wearing the early pattern hat with white cover and gilt metal CPO's badge. In her left hand she is holding a white pith helmet; this would have had a blue fold in the puggree and a gilt metal badge. (Imperial War Museum)

(**Below**) The officers' tropical hat (also issued to Wren senior rates later in the war), blouse and stockings. Gilt, rather than white plastic buttons were often used on the blouse. These, and the rank shoulder boards (here those of a First Officer) were easily detachable for laundering purposes.

(Right) Wren rating photographed in Alexandria, 1943, wearing the two-piece tropical uniform. The blouse has plastic naval buttons and is worn with the white-topped tropical cap, tropical skirt and a white money belt. (Imperial War Museum)

(Below) White canvas shoes with leather soles were worn with the tropical uniform. There were two patterns of shoe: that illustrated was a small sizing of the men's shoe with four pairs of lace eyelets and a low $^7/8$ in. heel. The other, slightly more feminine style had a higher $1^1/4$ in. heel and five pairs of eyelets; issue was dependent on availability.

(Right) Items of tropical uniform: the white-topped cap, white skirt, a blue money belt, 1943-dated white stockings, and "Blanco" for whitening shoes and cap. The skirt opening was on the left hip and incorporated a single pocket closed by a button; three further buttons, of white plastic or chromed metal, were used to close the skirt. This example was made in the Union of South Africa in 1943, and bears the U-and-broad-arrow government stamp.

QARNNS UNIFORMS

The Queen Alexandra's Royal Naval Nursing Service was the smallest of the three military nursing services: before 1939 it numbered only some 200 nursing sisters, with a supplementary reserve of civilian nursing sisters who were called up at the outbreak of war. Although a rapid expansion of the service was inevitable it was to remain relatively modest in size, with not more that 7,000 members. As the war progressed QARNNS nurses were to see service not only at home but also at naval stations abroad.

On the ward naval nursing sisters wore a dark blue working dress with a full-length buttoned front fastening. Worn with this dress were a white apron, a detachable white starched collar and red cuffs. For more formal wear a dark blue tippet (short cape) with narrow red trim, and a waistbelt, were worn. The tippet displayed the wearer's rank on the lower right front corner; this badge, bearing a crown and red cross, was originally woven in gold and silver wire, but during the war an economy version made with non-metallic thread was substituted. Senior nursing staff had a broad red trim to the tippet. The waistbelt, of a silk textured fabric, had a substantial round, white metal buckle bearing a crown and anchor surrounded by a laurel wreath. On her head the naval nursing sister wore a white veil, at the rear of which was embroidered a coronet insignia in blue. Black stockings and plain black shoes completed the uniform.

When not in ward dress, and befitting their officer status, QAs wore the same privately purchased uniform as WRNS officers. However, their rank insignia were worn as epaulettes rather than cuff rings; and the cap badge was the King's crown surmounting the anchor entwined with Queen Alexandra's cypher (the upper section of the rank badge), the cypher and anchor being enclosed by a narrow border.

For tropical use a lightweight white cotton dress was worn, with a white tippet with red trim, the waistbelt in white, and a white hat of a similar design to that worn by WRNS officers.

QARNNS rank	WRNS rank	Badge
Nursing Sister	Third Officer	Crown, anchor, red cross
Senior NS	Second Officer	Red bar beneath cross
Superintending Sister	First Officer	Red edge to badge
Matron	Chief Officer	Gold edge to badge
Principal Matron	Superintendent	Gold edge, 2 gold bars
Matron in Chief	Commandant	Doubled gold edge

(Left) HRH The Duchess of Kent, right, President of the WRNS - note greatcoat detail - chats with the QARNNS Reserve sister in charge of the sickbay at Rosyth. The sister wears the temperate climate ward dress of dark blue dress, red-piped dark blue tippet, white apron and collar, and red cuffs. (Imperial War Museum)

(Right) Detail of the badge worn by a QARNNS(R) sister. It is made up of the King's crown, a naval anchor entwined with Queen Alexandra's cypher, a red cross and the title "Reserve."

(Above) The tropical tippet on the left bears the badge of a Nursing Sister (Reserve); the broad red border identifies that on the right as being for Superintending Sisters and above - the ribbons are those of the Royal Red Cross and the Order of St John of Jerusalem. Also shown are the QARNNS veil, waist belt and cuffs.

(Left) Detail from a famous group photograph, taken in the UK before departure, showing the first contingent of Wrens to be drafted to the Far East in 1941. In the centre of the group a QARNNS sister in tropical uniform is surrounded by CPO Wrens, also in tropical clothing. (Imperial War Museum)

THE AUXILIARY TERRITORIAL SERVICE

T he ATS was created by Royal Warrant on 9 September 1938, notified in Army Order 199 of the same date. War seemed inevitable, and this time Britain would be prepared, on paper if not in reality. Experience in the Great War had proved that, once prejudices had been overcome, servicewomen were an invaluable asset. They were willing and able to undertake many men's jobs; even if they were not actually allowed to bear arms they could free a man to do so.

Responsibility for the formation of the ATS fell to three voluntary women's services: the First Aid Nursing Yeomanry, the Woman's Legion, and the Emergency Service (though some confusing retitling took place at intervals). These provided an officer cadre and, importantly, instructors for the ATS driving school. The majority were drawn from the middle classes, which provided educated, if not invariably suitable volunteers during the important formative period. Once the ATS had established itself officer selection was from the lower ranks, after an exhaustive selection procedure at the Duke of York's Headquarters in Chelsea.

The military had been unprepared for the influx of female

soldiers - some 17,000 had enlisted by September 1939 - and it was some time before all volunteers were issued with a complete uniform. It was not uncommon to see a few uniformed members parading alongside others wearing plain clothes and a black-on-blue "ATS" brassard. These women also received a small silver brooch, of the same design as the ATS cap badge.

Those who worked with the ATS were impressed by their capabilities; and acceptance was speeded by their achievements during their first Territorial Army summer camp in 1939. Small numbers served overseas with the BEF in France, 1939-40, and others were in Egypt by December 1940. By that date Anti-Aircraft Command was glad to take in 8,500 auxiliaries immediately, of 34,000 ATS volunteers then on strength.

A Defence Regulation of April 1941 saw the ATS granted full military status under the Army Act; and the conscription of women, under the National Service Act of December 1941, brought about a huge expansion - to some 200,000 auxiliaries and 6,000 officers, serving in more than 80 trades, by December 1943. Initially it had been envisaged that women would undertake only limited tasks such as clerical and motor transport duties. By the end of the war ATS women were serving in every theatre of operations and in countless, often demanding and hazardous roles, of which the most impressively visible on the Home Front were complete ATS searchlight units and mixed anti-aircraft batteries.

EARLY ATS SERVICE DRESS

With the formation of the ATS in 1938 a uniform for the new force had to be developed; and its design was influenced by the uniform then being worn by the First Aid Nursing Yeomanry and Motor Transport Training Corps.

The fabric was a lightweight khaki serge superior in quality to that used for men's uniforms, and lined throughout with khaki-brown cotton material. The tunic was of mid-thigh length, tailored open at the neck for wear with a shirt collar and tie, with two pleated patch breast pockets, and two flap-top internally hung pockets in the tunic skirt. It had epaulettes, on which were worn brass "ATS" titles (in keeping with the regimental titles then worn on male service dress); and a stitched-on half-belt at the rear waist. All tunic buttons were of brass General Service type.

The skirt, of the same material as the tunic, was a simple two-gore (-panel) design falling to mid-calf length.

ATS ranks pre-June 1941	Post-June 1941
Volunteer	Private
Chief Volunteer	Lance-Corporal
Sub-Leader	Corporal
Section Leader	Sergeant
Senior Leader	Warrant Officer II

(Left) The pattern of ATS service dress dating from 1939, worn by a former member of the FANY, whose motor transport companies had been merged with the ATS. To mark her former service this Sub-Leader wears FANY/WTS sleeve titles; and a leather (in this case male officer's pattern) chinstrap worn over the cap crown, replacing the cloth strap normally found on early caps. At this time ATS Other Ranks were called "Members", the title "Auxiliaries" not being adopted until July 1941.

(Below) Early pattern ATS shoes, in this case dated 1939. Note the shaped heel, and fabric laces finished with a crimped metal end.

(Right) Detail of the tunic and cap. Of note are the stitched lines on the peak and curtain of this early pattern cap.

(Below) Interior of an ATS officer's cap showing manufacturer's label, and its WTS (FANY) designation.

(Above) The Women's Transport Service (FANY) sleeve title, embroidered in red on buff. This was authorised to be worn on both sleeves by all ex-members of the FANY who had transferred to the ATS; it was not worn by those transferring after September 1941.

25

1941 PATTERN ATS SERVICE DRESS

This uniform, introduced in 1941, was a utility version of the earlier pattern. Despite some simplification of manufacture, the general lines of the tunic were greatly improved by the addition of a full belt at the waist. The most noticeably different features of the 1941 pattern tunic are the simplified breast pockets and flaps: plain, unpleated patch pockets with single- rather than three-point flaps.

(Left) This ATS Lance-Corporal attached to the Royal Signals is in transit to her next posting - perhaps to the rear headquarters of 21st Army Group in Normandy, where an ATS advance party had arrived by 28 July 1944; more than 6,200 auxiliaries were serving in NW Europe by the end of the year. She wears the 1941 pattern service dress uniform and the second pattern of cap, and carries the ATS handbag. The ATS holdall at her feet was introduced early in 1944 to replace the issue kitbag; its handles made it far easier to carry.

(Above) Details of the cap, pockets and insignia in close-up. The second pattern cap is of similar design to the first, but the card-stiffened peak and the curtain no longer show lines of stitching. A chinstrap of brown leather with a brass slider has replaced the earlier khaki cloth version. On both shoulders she proudly sports new British Troops in France sleeve insignia; and round her right shoulder a lanyard in the ATS colours of dark brown, beech brown and green. Above the left breast pocket she wears a Royal Signals badge, marking the unit to which she is attached. Authority for the wearing of these corps or regimental badges could only be given by the unit concerned and was not an entitlement.

(Right) An ATS handbag and a selection of its contents. Introduced in 1943, this was a welcome addition to the ATS kit list; apart from service necessities such as the AB64 paybook, it had room for some personal items such as cosmetics. Cosmetics in moderation were tolerated: it was understood that it was as important for morale for an ATS woman to look and feel her best as it was for a man to be clean shaven.

(**Left**) Detail of a late war version of the 1941 pattern tunic. As a further utility measure the brass GS buttons have been replaced by green "vegetable ivory" (plastic), and have been deleted altogether from the lower skirt pocket flaps. The bulldog insignia is that of Eastern Command.

(**Below**) Example of the type of label to be found on 1941 pattern skirts. The skirts were noticeably shorter than the earlier pattern, and were made up of four gores.

SKIRTS, A.T.S.
1941 PATTERN.

SIZE 1

Height—5ft. 1in. to 5ft. 2ins.

Waist under Skirt
23in. to 24in.

Hips over Skirt
34ins. to 35ins.

HECTOR POWE LTD
JANUARY 1943

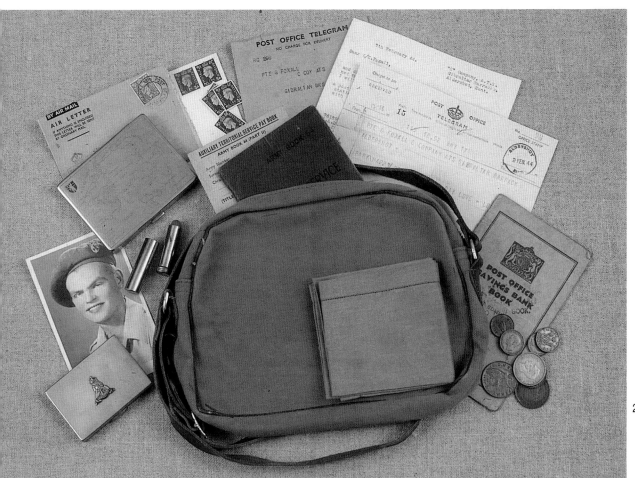

ATS PROVOST

Of necessity, the ATS provided their own Provost staff. As of 10 April 1941 the ATS had come under the Army Act and thereafter were fully subject to military law. There was no provision for the detention of auxiliaries, the highest punishment for a military offence being dismissal from His Majesty's service; civil offences were dealt with by the civil courts. This led to some anger among male soldiers, who could expect considerably more severe punishment for their crimes. An ATS deserter could not be detained, but a persistent offender would be discharged.

To cope with disciplinary problems within the ATS, volunteers were selected to train as military police. The first training course commenced at the Corps of Military Police depot at Mytchet in late 1941, the ATS Provost Wing being formed on 2 February 1942.

(Left) An ATS Provost Lance-Corporal wearing a 1941 pattern tunic, with the red-covered male Other Ranks' pattern of service dress cap, an "MP" brassard on the left arm, and a police whistle on its chain. She is carrying the Coat No.1A, a lightweight waterproof issued to MPs in lieu of the groundsheet/cape.

(Below) Detail of insignia: the brass ATS shoulder strap title, blue-on-red Provost sleeve title, command sleeve insignia of London District, Lance-Corporal's badge of rank, and red-on-blue Military Police brassard.

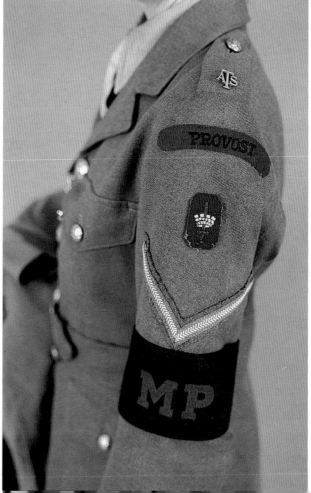

(Above) Military Police could always be recognised by their highly visible red cap covers. During the war the issue of the SD cap was restricted to certain units, including the Military Police and Guards regiments.

(Above right) Detail from a group photograph of an ATS Provost course at Mytchet, c.1943. Of note is the ATS Corporal in the centre of the front row, wearing the badge of the Corps of Military Police on her left breast. The ATS Provost did not normally wear this badge; they were Provost staff in their own right and as such were not attached to the CMP

(Right) The most common type of ATS shoe was this plain Oxford. Manufactured in red/brown pebble finish leather, it has five pairs of lace eyelets. The full sole and heel are of leather. ATS shoes of the WAAF apron-front style, but in brown leather, were also issued.

29

ATS OTHER RANKS' GREATCOAT

This coat was introduced as part of the major ATS uniform reforms which took place in 1941. The ATS 1941 pattern greatcoat replaced the 1939 and 1940 pattern men's greatcoats which had previously been issued to those auxiliaries requiring them. It could be said that the Army had taken two years to come to the conclusion that auxiliaries might require an overcoat, considering their much expanded war role. It was made of the same wool fabric as the male O/R's patterns, but the ATS were more fortunate in that their version was fully lined, unlike the half-lined coats of male personnel. In style the major difference in appearance of the ATS greatcoat is the absence of an adjusting half-belt at the rear waist; this was not considered necessary, as the coat did not need to expand to be worn over web equipment, and is correspondingly less full in the back. This gives the coat a much more fitted appearance; it is also cut for the female figure, being shaped at the bust and slightly waisted. As on the male infantry pattern greatcoat the pocket flaps are slightly angled, and the front is secured by ten large brass General Service buttons (the ATS having no regimental pattern button of their own). These were replaced by green plastic GS buttons on coats of late war manufacture. As with much of the ATS issue kit, the greatcoat fastens to the right (man's) side, with one dished plastic "jigger" button inside the left breast to balance the coat when buttoned up.

(Left) The auxiliary of c.1942 illustrated here is wearing the new greatcoat but still retains the early pattern stitched-peak cap with its cloth chinstrap. She is also wearing knitted wool stockings, which could only be considered as cold weather wear.

(Below) The greatcoat label, and the stamped marking showing the size and ATS designation. Also visible is part of the full-length white lining.

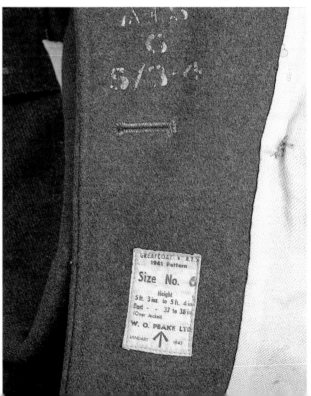

(Left) An ATS Provost Lance-Corporal wearing a man's pattern greatcoat, undergoing first aid training. In the early days, and later due to a shortage of the ATS pattern, many auxiliaries were issued with men's greatcoats. These were not an ideal solution, but were far superior to the gabardine raincoats initially issued to the ATS in the mistaken belief that they were adequate for the kind of duties originally envisaged for female personnel.

(Below) Detail of ATS wool knit stocking, and a label typical of the type found on these stockings.

ATS SHIRTS

(Right) A 1942-dated issue shirt shown with collar detached and front stud, and a 1941-dated tan coloured tie. The other shirt (far right), manufactured in 1945, is shown with its separate collar attached and with a 1944-dated green tie. The shade variations among these shirts and collars are random, not prescribed.

31

ATS BATTLEDRESS

It could be argued that if one event above all others was to cause the greatest changes in the design and development of the ATS uniform, then it was the introduction of mixed-sex batteries to Anti-Aircraft Command in 1941.

The existing service dress and raincoats were hopelessly inconvenient and inadequate on the often remote and windswept gun sites. Initially men's battledress was worn with the existing service shoes; while enabling the auxiliaries' tasks to be undertaken with a greater degree of comfort, this could only be considered as a stop-gap, as men's uniform sizing was clearly unsuitable. By the end of 1941 this had led to the introduction of BD tailored for the female figure, and of special ATS boots and gaiters far more practical for service in muddy gun sites than the light shoes.

(Left) This young auxiliary is wearing the early stitched-peak cap, and the newly issued ATS battledress uniform. The blouse largely mirrors the features of the man's BD blouse introduced in 1938. Distinctive features of the ATS blouse are its faced collar, allowing it to be worn open with a shirt and tie; and the softer "Saxony serge" fabric used in its manufacture (though examples exist of early trousers made in the standard serge material used for men's uniform).

(Right) Detail of the first pattern ATS BD blouse. The collar can be closed to the neck if required, by using the two hooks and eyes. Note the cloth chinstrap on the early cap; and the slip-on cloth epaulette titles, with "ATS" woven in black on khaki, which were ordered into use on BD throughout the Army at the outbreak of war - a cheaper printed version also existed. Titles are sometimes found cut down to a disc shape around the "ATS", and stitched directly to the epaulette.

BLOUSE
BATTLEDRESS
SERGE, A.T.S.
Size No. 4
Height: 5' 5" to 5' 6"
Bust: 37" to 40"
Waist: 29" to 32"

M. BELMONT & Co. Ltd.
1942

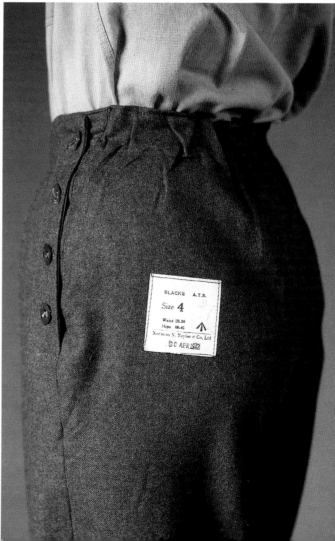

SLACKS A.T.S.
Size 4
Waist 29-30
Hips 40-41
Norman N. Taylor & Co. Ltd
20 APR 1942

(Left) ATS ankle boots and gaiters. The boots are most distinctive, having eleven pairs of eyelets and reaching quite high over the ankle. They are made of dimpled leather, and have the typical Army horseshoe heel and metal toe plate. The sole is normally found studded, depending on the auxiliary's trade - service drivers wore unstudded boots to prevent accidents being caused by the sole slipping on the pedals.

(Above right) The label on the early production ATS battledress blouse, this example made in 1942.

(Right) Detail of the first pattern slacks, showing the four-button fastening on the left side of the waist. Note also the elasticated rear waistband; and the label stitched to the outside, as on the men's battledress trousers.

ATS UTILITY PATTERN BD

Like their male comrades, the ATS had by the latter part of the war received their own simplified economy model of battledress uniform. The main objective of the simplification of the BD was to reduce the amount of materials used and the time taken in production.

The ATS utility pattern BD blouse is produced from the same Saxony serge as the 1941 pattern. The two major utility features are that all the buttons are exposed on the front, cuffs, and pockets; and the pleats have been deleted from the breast pockets. The collar is still faced with serge, allowing it to be worn open; but only a single hook and eye is provided to close the collar if required.

On the utility pattern slacks the number of buttons on the side closure has been reduced from four to three; however, improvements include an adjustable elasticated tab at the waist, and tabs at the bottom of the trouser legs allowing them to be drawn in tight when wearing anklets. The tabs have two button positions of adjustment plus a retaining button to secure them when not in use.

(Left) Shown here are the modified ATS battledress blouse and slacks, c.1945. Note the exposed buttons on the blouse and the tabs at the bottom of the trouser legs.

(Below) Also noteworthy are the boots, which by 1945 had been reduced in height from eleven to eight eyelets. This was a logical modification; the 1941 pattern was taller than practically necessary, wasting leather while simply adding bulk to the bottom of the leg when wearing anklets.

(Left) The ATS "hospital blue" version of the utility BD blouse. This was worn by auxiliaries while convalescing in military hospitals, with a matching two-gore skirt. This example has a conventional manufacturer's label (L.Harris Ltd.) with the designation "Blouse Hospital/ A.T.S." and is dated 1945.

(Above) Label from the utility version of the ATS BD blouse. This was located on the internal breast pocket.

(Left) Detail of the printed shoulder title in the ATS colours of brown, beech and green, first issued in October 1944 - this is the most common type of QM issue title. Also shown is the lanyard, again in the ATS colours, which was normally worn on the right shoulder by all ranks. Auxiliaries serving in AA Command were allowed to substitute the white Royal Artillery lanyard, a sign of the esteem in which they were held.

CONVERTED BATTLEDRESS

Due to shortages of the ATS Saxony serge battledress, many ATS auxiliaries were of necessity issued male pattern BD. Often only minimal alterations were made, the main modification being the opening of the collar and re-facing it with serge. (By contrast, the example of the converted blouse ilustrated at left has clearly been completely re-tailored to conform to the female figure. While retaining the original label on the inside breast pocket, a new and smaller label showing the woman's sizing and "Modified" has been stitched below it.)

The khaki beret, once the distinctive headgear of certain officers, the Reconnaissance Corps and infantry Motor Battalions, had by 1945 become the widely tolerated alternative to the less attractive general service cap. In the case of the ATS the beret was official issue for field wear. It was worn with the badge mounted on a teardrop-shaped backing in the service colours.

(Left) This auxiliary, as she might have appeared in occupied Germany in 1945, is wearing a 1944-dated khaki beret with ATS badge and backing; a converted man's battledress blouse; and the late war ATS slacks with button-adjusted trouser bottoms for use when wearing anklets. The serge facing on the open-tailored collar can be clearly seen.

(Below) The label from the late pattern "Slacks, ATS". Unlike the label on the earlier slacks this was positioned internally.

SLACKS, A.T.S.
SIZE 1
WAIST 23ins. to 24ins.
HIPS 34ins. to 35ins.
GORBY, PALMER & STEWART
1945.

(Below) The brass cap badge of ATS Other Ranks, mounted on the service-coloured backing cloth introduced in 1945

(Right) ATS work shirt manufactured in a khaki fabric. It has an attached collar, a half-fly front secured by three buttons, and a small open-top pocket on the left breast. The cuff and front buttons are made of a synthetic rubber compound. Used as a general work shirt in temperate climates, it was also often used in tropical areas.

The Royal Artillery "sweetheart brooch" worn on the tie is an unofficial adornment. Such pins, although scorned by authority, were often worn throughout the women's services, adding a feminine touch to the otherwise drab uniform.

(Left) A selection of ATS tie bars, sweetheart brooches, and an ATS silver and enamel ring. These popular items were purchased for the individual's own use or as gifts for family or friends.

EARLY ATS OFFICER'S SERVICE DRESS

At the outbreak of war in September 1939 the ATS officer was wearing a uniform that differed little from those of the sister services - the First Aid Nursing Yeomanry and the Motor Transport Training Corps - the main distinction being insignia and, in the case of the MTTC,

headgear. All were ultimately styled after the male officer's service dress uniform, and were acquired by the same means - private purchase from military tailors. This left scope for a degree of individual choice by the discerning customer, and in the case of shirts, ties, stockings and shoes some variation in colour and fabric would depend on preference and purchasing power. Although a uniform grant of £40.00 was provided, this barely covered essential uniform items. Additions such as Sam Browne belts and, later, coloured field service caps were optional. The uniform made few allowances for femininity. The tunic buttoned on the man's side; this was felt necessary, as any decorations would be worn on the left side.

ATS Officer Rank Structure 1938-1945

1938-1941	Post-June 1941	Army rank
Chief Controller	Chief Controller	Major-General
Senior Controller	Senior Controller	Brigadier
Controller	Controller	Colonel
Chief Commandant	Chief Commandant	Lieut.Col.
Senior Commandant	Senior Commandant	Major
Company Commander	Junior Commandant	Captain
Junior Cdr.	Subaltern	Lieutenant
Company Assistant	2nd Subaltern	2nd Lieut.

(**Above**) The early pattern of uniform being worn with the Regular Army rank insignia introduced in June 1941; the Major's crown identifies a Senior Commandant. The optional Sam Browne waist belt is being worn here in place of the cloth tunic belt; its shoulder strap component was not worn by ATS officers.

(**Right**) An ATS Junior Commander, c.1939. Rayon stockings and brown leather gloves are typical officers' additions to the basic uniform.

ATS OFFICER'S GREATCOAT

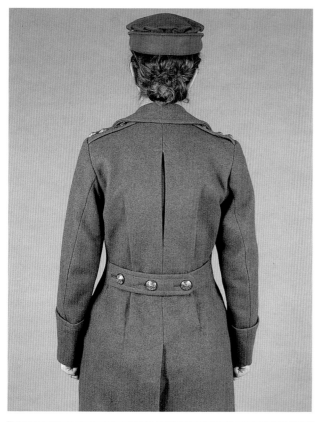

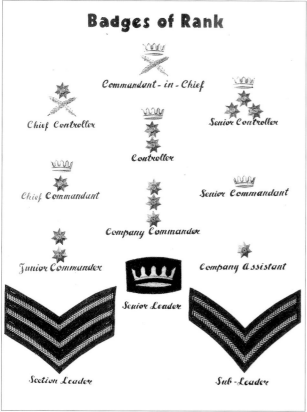

Badges of Rank

Commandant - in - Chief

Chief Controller

Senior Controller

Controller

Chief Commandant

Senior Commandant

Company Commander

Junior Commander

Company Assistant

Senior Leader

Section Leader

Sub - Leader

(Left) Prior to the introduction of the Regular Army badges of rank in June 1941 the ATS had their own unique badges. These were in bronze from 1938 until February 1940, and gilt from then until June 1941. Shown here is the ATS rank structure dating from early 1940, when a gilt crown coronet replaced the earlier plain bronze wreath. (Imperial War Museum)

(Above left & above) A Junior Commander wearing the ATS officer's greatcoat. Made of waterproofed khaki drab wool melton, this double-breasted "lancer"-style coat was secured at the front by two rows of four gilt or brass GS buttons, and buttoned to the male side, left over right. Indeed, it was almost identical to the male officer's coat except for the absence of

the latter's "sword slit" just above the left pocket. As with service dress, the quality and colour of the lining varied according to personal taste, a three-quarter length lining of red or blue silk being quite common. Smart and functional, the coat was worn only at the CO's discretion: officers were required to wear their greatcoats when O/Rs were also dressed in theirs, and it was forbidden for an officer to parade in a greatcoat when they were not being worn by the O/Rs. On parade it was usually worn fully buttoned to the neck (as e.g. page 30).

The rear of the greatcoat shows the three-buttoned half-belt, and the box pleat running down the centre of the back. Note also the gauntlet cuffs; these were deleted on later patterns.

OFFICER'S AUSTERITY PATTERN SERVICE DRESS

ATS officers' service dress was affected to the same degree as male officers' SD by various utility measures introduced to reduce the cost of manufacture and the materials consumed. These modifications included the deletion of the external lower pockets from the tunic skirt and the substitution of internal pockets, and removal of the pleats from the breast pocket and the ornamental false cuffs from the sleeves.

(Left) ACI 501 of March 1942 detailed the changes required to save material in the officers' uniform. Not all the requirements were always applied, as can be seen by the tunic being worn by this ATS Junior Commander. She is wearing government issue rayon stockings rather than the more common lisle pattern. She carries a copy of the 1941 *Regulations for the Auxiliary Territorial Service.*

(Below) As a concession to femininity tunics were often lined with coloured silk or similar materials, as in this example. Note also the officer's collar badges; and the breast badge, showing that this ATS officer was attached to the Royal Army Ordnance Corps.

(**Left**) The same pattern of tunic badged for the Women's Transport Service (FANY). While retaining the early pleated breast pocket it has internal pockets in the skirt, with no buttons on the flaps. The sleeves are plain, with no false cuff.

(**Below**) Detail of the bronze ATS officer's cap badge; this is identical in design to the brass badge worn by O/Rs, but normally retained by flat bronze clips bent back to secure it in place.

(**Right**) An officer's quality moleskin cap, with officer's pattern leather chinstrap and bronze finish ATS badge.

ATS OFFICER, SCOTTISH COMMAND

In early 1945 the Board of Trade lifted its restrictions applying to the tailoring of officers' uniforms. From that time tailors could accept orders for uniforms of the pre-1942 pattern, providing facilities and materials were adequate to meet demand. There was no obligation for officers holding austerity pattern uniforms to purchase new uniforms, and both patterns could be worn concurrently.

(Left & below) This Senior Commandant is wearing a tunic manufactured in 1945 but of the pre-1942 pattern, with pleated breast pockets, bellows skirt pockets with buttoned flaps, and false cuffs. The tartan skirt is non-regulation but was authorised for private purchase by ATS ranks serving in infantry training depots of Scottish Command. The tartan worn was that of the particular regiment stationed at the depot, which in this officer's case is the Hunting Stuart sett of The Royal Scots. The Sam Browne waist belt and coloured field service cap are optional private-purchase items.

COLOURED FIELD SERVICE CAPS

(**Right**) ATS officer's coloured field service cap. Manufactured in a fine moleskin fabric, it has bronzed buttons, and the ATS officer's cap badge backed with coloured felt. The body and curtain are of dark brown with green piping on the curtain edge and crown seams. The top fold of the crown, hidden here, is of beech brown fabric. Note also the details of the detachable shirt collar, secured by a stud; and the collar pin fixed under the tie knot, frequently worn by officers and auxiliaries in the 1940s.

(**Left**) Private purchase ATS coloured field service caps. From top to bottom: a fine quality officer's cap with bronze badge and buttons; an auxiliary's cap with brass badge and buttons, the beech brown top fold just visible at the rear corner of the crown; and the Royal Artillery coloured FS cap in blue and red, as worn with some pride by auxiliaries attached to AA Command and other RA units.

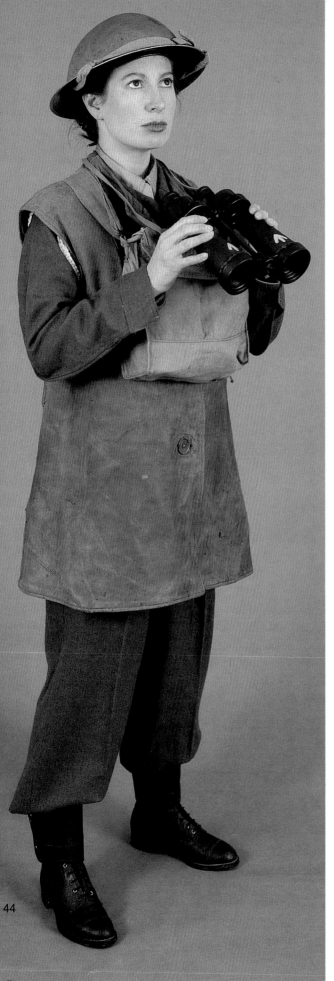

ATS LEATHER JERKINS

The leather jerkin was not considered as being normal workwear, but as an item of cold weather clothing to be used when the greatcoat proved too restrictive. Being three-quarter length and sleeveless it was ideal for heavy labour during colder weather.

The first specifically ATS pattern of jerkin, introduced at the end of 1941, had a full skirt and an adjustable buckled half-belt at the rear. On the second pattern the skirt wasreduced and the half-belt deleted. As a utility measure jerkins were increasingly made up from smaller panels of leather, giving some examples a patchwork appearance. On both patterns the buttons fastened on the female side.

As with the men's pattern, a camouflaged version of the ATS jerkin was also issued. Made in the same style as the belted early version, it had a lightly spray-painted green camouflage pattern on the leather surface. (Again as with the men's pattern, the contrast between the shades was not striking and the camouflage effect was minimal.)

(Left) This ATS "gunner" attached to a mixed AA battery is wearing the early pattern of jerkin. The steel helmet was a necessity, as gun sites were frequently targets for enemy aircraft. The service respirator is worn on the chest in the ready position. ATS boots and leather anklets complete the outfit.

(Below) Rear view of the leather jerkin showing the adjustable half-belt; and the method of securing the respirator haversack when worn in the ready position. Note the white Royal Artillery lanyard, proudly worn on the right shoulder by ATS auxiliaries serving with Anti-Aircraft Command.

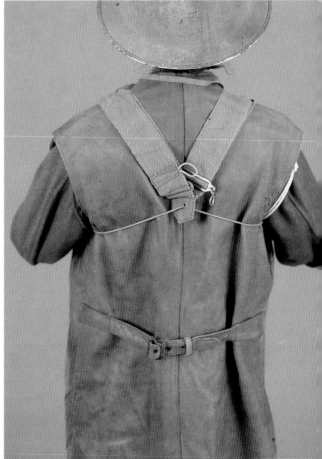

(**Left**) An auxiliary serving in NW Europe, 1945, wears a late war jerkin with its shorter skirt; this pattern does not have the rear half-belt. Note also her general service cap worn with the ATS badge and backing.

(**Below**) The label stitched inside the right flap of this late production ATS jerkin.

JERKINS, LEATHER
A.T.S.

Size No. 1

Height 5ft 1ins to 5ft 4ins
Bust   34ins to 36ins

H. WINTER
London
1945

(**Right**) The long hose version of the service respirator. This pattern was often issued to such trades as predictor numbers, who had to wear the haversack to the rear of the left side to prevent it becoming snagged or causing an obstruction in a tight working environment. It was worn horizontally in the small of the back with the opening to the wearer's left.

"TEDDY BEAR COAT"

From an early stage of the war the resources of manpower available to Anti-Aircraft Command came under intense pressure - by December 1940, at the height of the Luftwaffe's Blitz on British cities, the Command was already 19,000 men short. Throughout the war a steady flow of men were posted away to artillery units of the field armies, and this loss had to be made up somehow. It was therefore decided that women would fill operational posts on AA sites (ATS girls had been with the Command since the outbreak of war, but previously only in clerical and administrative roles). The first call for female volunteers for mixed AA batteries went out in the late summer of 1940. The experiment proved an undoubted success, with the women doing every task with the exception of actually serving the guns. Many mixed batteries were soon to become operational, and from the spring of 1941 the ATS were to man and run their own searchlight sites.

Often exposed to extreme winter weather during basically static duties on operational sites, ATS personnel were issued the "Smock AA (Wool Pile) ATS", more generally called the "teddy bear coat".

(Left) An AA artillery predictor crew number has a welcome brew at her post; she wears the "teddy bear coat" over as much additional clothing as can be crammed on under it. The tall collar of the "Smock AA" is strapped up, and wool-lined "Shearling" mittens are worn. The Mk II helmet has a camouflaged anti-gas hood attached more as protection from the elements than from enemy vesicants.

(Below) Detail of the wool pile fabric, and the leather-backed bracket fixed on the left hip of the smock for attaching, amongst other items, a service issue torch.

(Bottom) Label in a "Smock AA (Wool Pile) ATS".

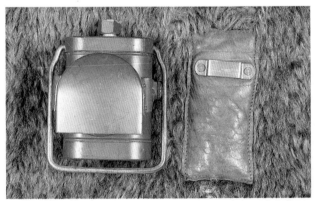

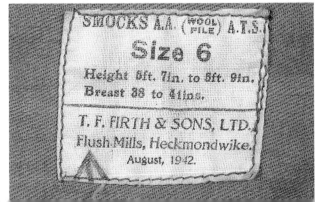

SMOCKS A.A. (WOOL PILE) A.T.S.

Size 6

Height 5ft. 7in. to 5ft. 9in.
Breast 38 to 41ins.

T. F. FIRTH & SONS, LTD.
Flush Mills, Heckmondwike.
August, 1942.

ATS PT KIT

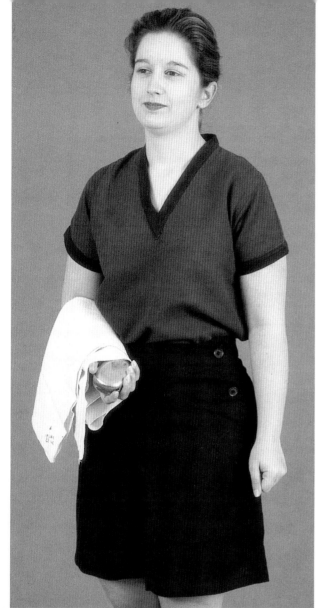

This was introduced in 1943, and no doubt represented the official "tidying up" of one of many loose ends of the dress code. What had previously been an *ad hoc* arrangement was replaced by a practical three-piece sports outfit, produced in the immediately recognisable ATS colours of beech and chocolate brown, the colours doubtless enhancing *esprit de corps* at sports events.

Worn by all auxiliaries during training, the PT kit was normally withdrawn upon posting; however, those women sent to mixed AA batteries were allowed to retain their kit. The PT vest was also issued to auxiliaries working in bakeries.

The short-sleeved vest in beech-colour Aertex fabric came in two patterns: a simple collarless V-neck (believed to be the earlier pattern), and a buttoned neck with collar.

The shorts ("Skirt, Divided, ATS") were made in a chocolate brown fabric, and secured by button fastenings on the left side. They have a generous pleated cut allowing great freedom of movement. Worn under the skirt were matching brown Aertex "Knickers PT", elasticated at waist and leg for reasons of modesty given the loose cut of the "Skirt, Divided".

(Left) The PT vest with collarless V-neck. The beech brown top has chocolate brown trim to the neck and sleeves. Note the buttoned fastening on the left hip of the "Skirt, Divided, ATS"; this example was manufactured in 1943 by Woolland Bros.Ltd. The outfit would be completed by brown plimsolls of the standard Army pattern, and khaki ATS ankle socks.This auxiliary carries an issue towel dated 1943, and a commercial pattern of soap dish.

(Below left) "Knickers, PT".

(Below) Variation of the PT vest with collar and buttoned neck. This physical training instructor holds a 1943 edition of *Games and Sports in the Army,* issued by the Army Sport Control Board and listing rules for all games played in the Army.

47

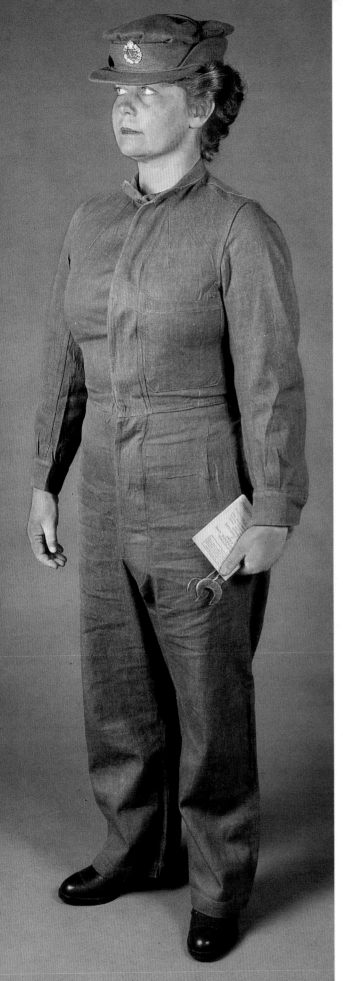

OVERALLS, COMBINATION, ATS

For those employed on particularly dirty tasks, such as vehicle mechanics, the "Overalls, Combination, Denim, ATS" were issued. These were one-piece overalls made of heavy green denim material. They had a full fly front secured by metal buttons; a small open-top pocket on the left breast; a tool pocket measuring 14 in. by 2 in. in the right side leg seam; and a half-belt at the rear.

During the early war years the two-piece men's denim coveralls (often referred to as "denim BD") were often issued to the ATS. Poorly fitting even on the male frame, they tended to look ridiculous on women.

(Left) The ATS denim overalls worn by a driver/mechanic serving at the Motor Transport Training Company, Camberley. Like all drivers she wears the chinstrap over the crown of the cap.

(Below) A typical example of size and manufacturer's stamp in the second pattern cap worn by the mechanic.

(Right) An ATS vehicle mechanic working on the engine of a lend-lease Ford GPW Jeep. She wears "Overalls, Combination, Denim, ATS", a leather jerkin, and a second pattern cap.

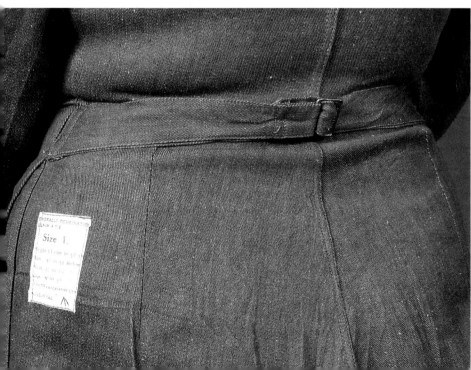

(Left) The rear of the overalls, showing the adjustable half-belt and label. The belt was occasionally worn fastened at the front of the overalls. Also visible at the side is one of the slash openings allowing access to the slacks when worn beneath. This slash tended to bulge open when the wearer adopted any position other than straight upright.

ATS WORKWEAR

In order to prevent unnecessary soiling of an auxiliary's uniform clothing while employed in supporting roles such as storekeepers and ordnance personnel, overall dresses were supplied.

The first pattern, dating from 1941, closely resembled the type of overall generally worn in the 1940s by housewives and women cleaners in all walks of civilian life. It had long sleeves closed at the cuffs by a button; it covered the torso and legs to mid-calf length, and was open at the neck with a simple shawl collar effect. The front panels could be wrapped across the body either left or right uppermost, and secured by two tie tapes at the waist; wartime photographs show auxiliaries wearing them wrapped to either side. A small open-top patch pocket was set on each side of the front just below the waist. Examples of this garment exist in both a tan coloured cotton drill fabric and green denim - the same material as used in the one-piece combination overall, page 48. (A navy blue version of this overall was used by the WAAF, see page 83.)

By 1943 the wrap-over pattern seems to have been superseded by a new "frock" type overall in khaki cotton fabric. This pattern had a half-length front closure secured with six exposed plastic buttons, of the pattern found on men's denims, secured detachably by split pins or split rings. An adjustable rear half-belt was secured by two buttons; and there was a small open-top patch pocket on the lower right front.

(Below) The early pattern of wrap-over overall, in this case made of tan cotton material; this was much lighter weight than the denim version. Note pocket and cuff detail.

(Right) The heavier version in green denim material, worn by a storewoman auxiliary, who carries a copy of SO Book 130 in which she has listed her stores inventory.

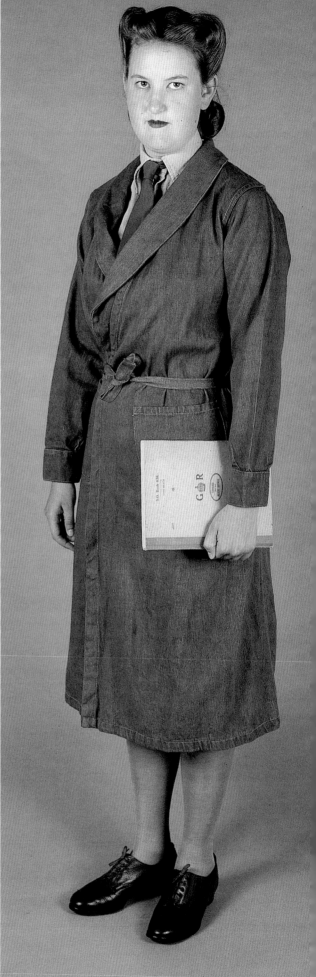

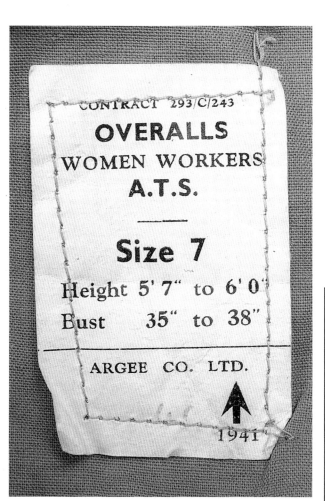

The ATS cook's overall closely resembled the "Overalls, Women Workers, ATS", being of a wrap-over design and secured by tie tapes. It differed in having short sleeves, and a single pocket on the left side only; and was made of a white cotton drill material. This garment was often worn with a small cook's hat or headscarf of the same fabric. It was designed for wear by tradeswomen qualified as cooks, and was not issued to other auxiliaries, such as those who found themselves temporarily on cookhouse fatigues.

(Below) An ATS cook wearing the wrap-over cook's overalls. She also wears an Army Catering Corps "sweetheart" pin on her tie.

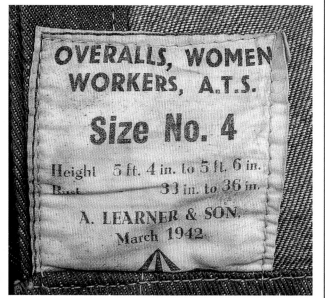

(Above, top) Detail of 1941-dated label on the tan cotton overalls, positioned inside the lower right front.

(Above) The label on the green denim overalls.

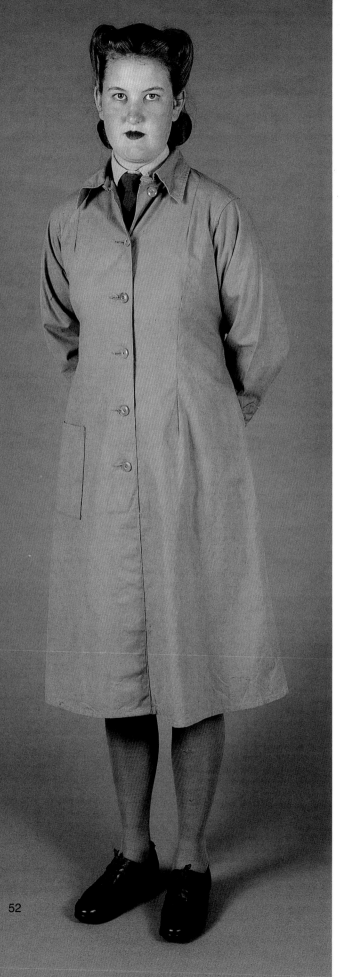

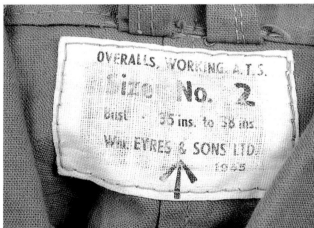

OVERALLS, WORKING, A.T.S.
Size No. 2
Bust - 35 ins. to 38 ins.
Wm. EYRES & SONS LTD
1945

(**Left**) This auxiliary is wearing the second, "frock" pattern of working overalls with a more practical buttoned front closure.

(**Above, top**) Detail of the half-belt on the rear of the frock-type overalls. This was occasionally buttoned to the front, adding a little flair to otherwise plain lines.

(**Above**) The label from the frock-type overalls, this example dated 1945.

ATS DESPATCH RIDER

One of the earliest ATS trades other than clerical and domestic was that of Despatch Rider. Auxiliaries proved well suited to this important task, and handled their motorcycles with impressive expertise.

During the early days no specialist clothing was issued, motorcycle riders wearing service dress with slacks and the ordinary peaked cap. This uniform was soon supplemented, for obvious practical reasons, with boots, puttees, and the early pattern of "pulp" crash helmet. The helmet offered some protection, but was inadequate during a period when there were, inevitably, many serious road accidents due to the universal "blackout" - the drastic reduction of street and vehicle lighting as a security precaution against enemy night bombing. The introduction of the Mk I despatch rider's steel helmet in July 1943 was therefore welcomed; this was similar to the Royal Armoured Corps helmet but with the addition of a full leather side curtain, as used on the pulp helmet. The unsuitably restrictive nature of the ATS slacks also led to the substitution of knickerbockers - knee-length breeches cut full in the thigh and seat, much more suitable for riding.

(Left) An ATS Corporal Despatch Rider, wearing the early pattern of tunic modified by the addition of a belt. An early economy measure (also often seen on WAAF tunics) is the use of separate cuff sections on the sleeve, allowing for the use of smaller lengths of material. This "Don-R" also wears knickerbockers, boots, and puttees wound in the reversed "mounted" style. She carries the early pulp helmet and MT gloves.

(Below left) Detail of the label on the rear of the knickerbockers; their use was not restricted to motorcycle riders.

(Below) Detail of the knickerbockers with their leg fastenings; MT goggles; Mk I steel crash helmet; and three variations of ATS issue MT gloves - (left to right) Canadian-made gloves, standard pattern brown gloves, and natural colour hide gloves. All three types were issued to ATS drivers and bear women's W-prefix serial numbers.

Knickerbockers, Serge.
Motor Drivers, A.T.S.

Size No. 2

Height 5ft 1in—5ft 3in
Waist   28in—30in
Hips   39in—41in

L. HARRIS LTD.
January, 1942.

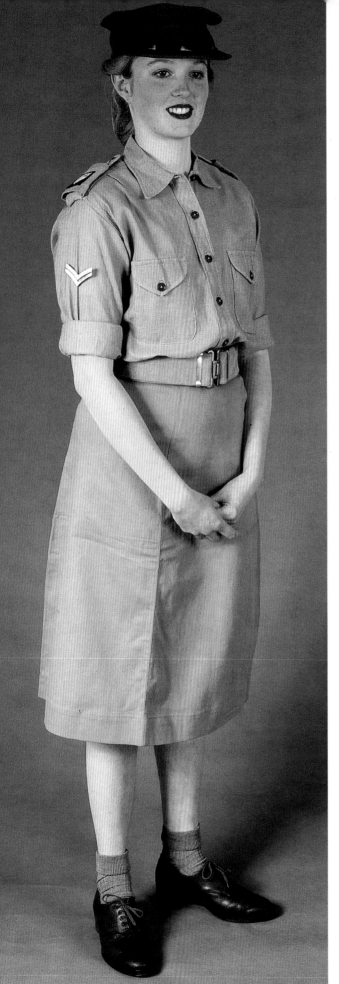

ATS KHAKI DRILL CLOTHING

Tropical clothing for the ATS closely followed the designs already in use by their male comrades. It was manufactured in pale khaki cotton drill, or in "Aertex" fabric - a lightweight open weave material ideally suited to use in hot climates. The heavier close weave drill was used for items subject to greater wear, such as skirts and slacks, while the Aertex was used for shirts and jackets. While ties were not required in tropical regions, khaki lisle stockings were supposed to be worn; in fact they were frequently dispensed with for reasons of comfort.

While in transit to tropical regions ATS personnel were issued pith helmets; but while these were worn on the troopships they were withdrawn again on arrival in theatre. This left the ATS with only their service dress cap as headgear.

(Left) This ATS Corporal serving with the Eighth Army in Italy is wearing the standard tropical uniform for auxiliaries: the SD cap, Aertex shirt, 1937 pattern web belt, and khaki drill skirt worn with ankle socks and shoes in preference to stockings.

(Below) The plastic cap badge as worn on the SD cap. Plastic badges were introduced as an economy measure in 1942, as part of an effort to save on the quantity of brass being used unnecessarily for items that could be made from non-strategic materials.

(**Right**) The Aertex shirt with its two patch pockets and epaulettes, worn here with slip-on Eighth Army formation badges, and brass pin-on Corporal's chevrons. There was a tendency for all insignia worn on clothing which required frequent laundering to be made in easily detachable forms.

(**Left**) Detail of the Aertex fabric used for the shirt, this example dated 1943. Note the open weave, providing good ventilation.

ATS KD BUSH JACKET

The ATS khaki drill bush jacket, like the larger family of Army KD, is made of a light Aertex fabric. It is very similar to the male bush jacket, and in the case of the example illustrated, identical to the jungle green example on the opposite page.

A relative latecomer by comparison with KD shirts and skirts, the bush jacket's principle advantage over the KD shirt lay in its considerably greater degree of comfort. Being loosely cut and often worn without a shirt, it allowed air to circulate freely around the body. In practice its scale of issue was mainly limited to India and East Africa.

(Left) This auxiliary serving in India in the last month of the war displays the khaki Aertex bush jacket worn with the KD skirt and service dress cap. During the heat of the day sleeves were worn rolled up, but were ordered rolled down at dusk as a precaution against malaria infection from mosquito bites. She is reading a July 1945 copy of *Victory* magazine, which was published for India Command.

(Below) The manufacturer's label on the ATS Aertex KD bush jacket, this example made in India by Dawoodson in 1945.

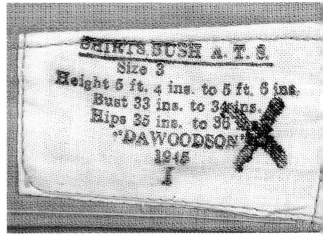

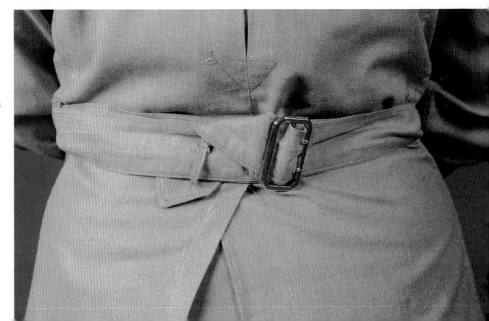

(Right) Detail of the removable belt and brass two-prong buckle. Here it is worn buckled back to the rear, a less restrictive alternative style.

ATS JG BUSH JACKET

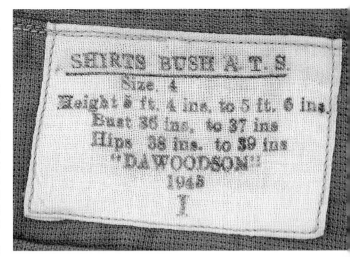

In the Far Eastern theatre the light tan-coloured khaki drill clothing initially worn by the garrisons which faced the 1942 Japanese offensives was obviously unsuitable for jungle combat, being far too visible. This problem was partially solved by dyeing the KD uniform green to provide a stop-gap jungle uniform. Contracts for a purpose-made alternative were placed with Indian manufacturers, resulting in the "jungle green" (JG) uniform. Priority was naturally given to providing clothing for combat troops, and most ATS personnel in the Far East saw out the war dressed in the tan KD.

It was therefore not until 1945 that the first ATS JG clothing appeared. The ATS jungle green Aertex bush jacket has patch breast pockets with buttoned single-point flaps, and two internally hung skirt pockets with external flaps. The fabric waist belt is stitched to the tunic at the back to prevent loss, and secures at the front with a two-prong brass buckle; the cuffs are secured by a single button; and epaulettes are provided for the display of rank or unit insignia.

(Below) The ubiquitous bush hat, made of compressed felt. This headgear was the best then available for use in tropical forest terrain, and was popular with the troops. A press stud on the left side allowed the brim to be fastened up, "Digger" style. The crown of the hat was shaped to the wearer's personal taste, with many unsoldierly variations being encountered. Formation badges were often attached (when out of the front line) to one or both sides of the cotton puggree, or to the lower surface of the left brim when it was worn fastened up. The hat's jaunty appearance was also popular with female personnel.

(Right) The ATS JG bush jacket as worn in the Far East theatre of operations, with matching slacks, and the felt bush hat which was the standard field headgear for most personnel in this theatre. The label in this bush jacket (right above) includes the standard "I" - for Indian manufacture - below the date 1945.

NURSE'S SERVICE DRESS

Established as a crown service in 1902, Queen Alexandra's Imperial Military Nursing Service provided the backbone of the Army's nursing services. In September 1939 the QAIMNS had fewer than 700 Regular members; but at the outbreak of war these numbers were bolstered by the mobilisation of the QAIMNS (Reserve) and the Territorial Army Nursing Service (TANS). Nurses from all three components were to serve on all fronts, in both base and field hospitals, often in difficult and dangerous circumstances - casualty clearing stations were usually in close proximity to the front lines.The skills of the Army's nurses were supplemented by those of the civilian members of the Voluntary Aid Detachments (VADs).

The scarlet and grey uniform initially worn by the nursing services proved increasingly difficult to obtain, rationing having taken its toll of available fabric. In order to ease procurement difficulties it was decided that all Army nurses would wear the khaki uniform as worn by ATS officers with effect from 1 January 1944. Cap and collar badges of the individual nursing service were worn, as was a lanyard in the nursing services' scarlet and grey.

Nurses had enjoyed officer status since 1904. In 1941 the King's commission, and the appropriate rank badges, were granted to all Army nurses in the following equivalent ranks.

Nursing Service rank structure 1941-45:

Nursing Services	Army equivalent
Matron-in-Chief	Brigadier
Chief Principal Matron	Colonel
Principal Matron	Lieutenant Colonel
Matron	Major
Senior Sister	Captain
Sister	Lieutenant

(Left) Items of a QAIMNS(R) Sister's service dress, 1943. Note the "Norfolk" cut of the early grey and scarlet tunic; cap and collar badges; and the ATS-style cap in grey, introduced in 1943 to replace the old brimmed "schoolgirl hat".

(**Left & right**) A Nursing Sister of the Territorial Army Nursing Service, 1944, wearing a utility version of the ATS officer's service dress. The nurses' pride in their old scarlet and grey uniform is reflected in the colours of the nursing services' prominent double lanyard.

(**Above**) The Territorial Army Nursing Service badge of office in its case of issue; the emblem is of sterling silver, on a scarlet and grey ribbon.

(**Above right**) Detail of the collar and lapels, showing the TANS collar badges and the manufacturer's label of Boyd Cooper, an established firm having strong links with the nursing services.

NURSE'S WARD DRESS

Ward dress (daily work dress) for nursing officers consisted of a grey smock-type dress fastening at the front with small white buttons concealed by a fly. The lower half of the front closure was offset to the left of the centre line; the long sleeves were fastened at the cuff by two buttons. On the left breast was a small U-shaped patch pocket, and on the right a long narrow patch pocket suitable for a thermometer or pen. At the neck was a detachable starched collar of white cotton. The general styling of this dress mirrored that of all contemporary nursing service uniforms, both civilian and military.

A white apron was worn for duties which might soil the dress; this was a simple wrap-around skirt with a bib front secured at the back by tie tapes. The traditional veil headdress bore an embroidered service emblem at its rear point.

No military nursing uniform was complete without the traditional service-coloured tippet, the small cape worn over the nurse's shoulders; or, in colder weather, a long "corridor cape" which was worn secured across the chest by two X-straps.

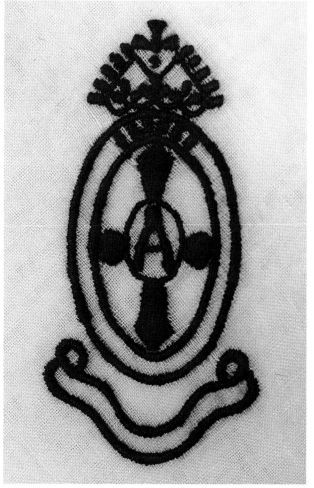

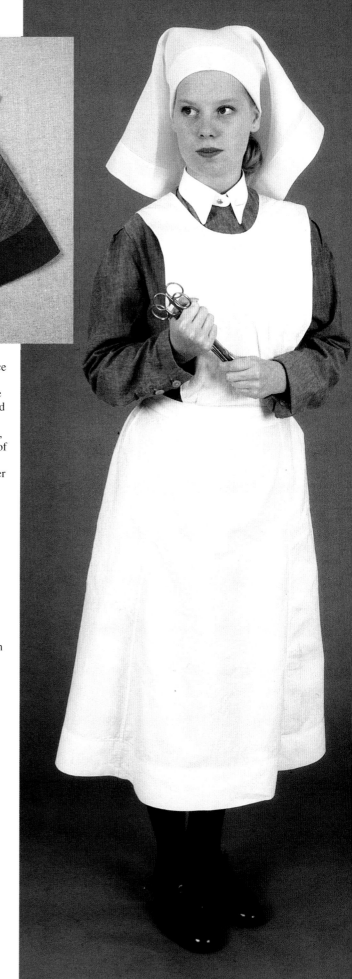

(Above) Army nursing service capes. Left, the rear of the scarlet QAIMNS tippet - note the traditional centrally placed cloth "rose" found on all nursing service tippets. Right, in scarlet and grey, the front of the QAIMNS(R) tippet. An identical cape but with a silver "T" on each front point was worn by the TANS. Also shown are the corresponding shoulder boards of rank for a Sister of the QAIMNS (left) and QAIMNS Reserve.

(Right) Ward dress worn with the white apron. A functional form of dress for base hospitals, this uniform was unsuited to use in field hospitals, particularly those in North Africa.

(Far left) A Nursing Sister of the QAIMNS wearing the grey ward dress with scarlet tippet. The offset front fastening of the dress below the waist can be seen in this image. Queen Alexandra decided on the service colours of grey and scarlet when the service received its Royal Warrant in 1902.

(Left) The embroidered badge of the QAIMNS on the back of the nurse's veil. Other services wore their own device in the same position.

NURSE'S FIELD DRESS

In 1944 a revised design of the nurse's ward dress was introduced, easier to produce and requiring less upkeep in terms of laundering - gone was the starched white collar which needed frequent and time-consuming laundering and ironing. Manufactured in the familiar grey cotton (the traditional colour, selected by Florence Nightingale for nurses' uniforms in 1854), this dress is far more functional than its predecessor.

Designated the "field force dress", it has detachable sleeves, large patch pockets on each thigh, and larger breast pockets. At the waist is a belt of matching grey fabric with a prongless chromed buckle. Rank is displayed on detachable epaulettes in service colours. Like the previous ward dress this pattern is fly-fronted, with concealed plastic buttons; but the front closure is straight, without the left offset at the waist.

(Left) "Dress, Field Force, Nursing Officers", worn here by a member of the QAIMNS(R), with the sleeves removed. Note the full length fly front, pockets and waistbelt.

(Below) Label in the field force dress, this example made in 1944 by E.Garner & Co. It has been overstamped with "APPROVED" and a WD arrow in violet ink.

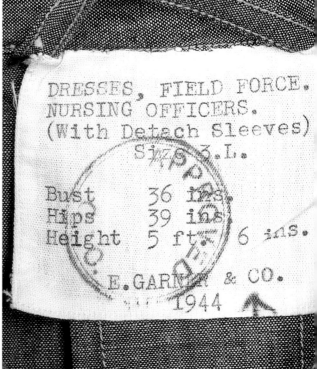

(Above) Each of the three Army Nursing Services had its own unique insignia; shown here are the emblems worn as cap and collar badges, each surmounted by the King's crown. From left to right:

QAIMNS bi-metal, bearing the title in full and with the motto "Sub Cruce Candida" - "under the sign of the white cross." This design was approved in 1905 by King Edward VII, the motto and Cross of Dannebrog being chosen by his Danish queen, Alexandra.

TANS, found in bi-metal and silver; it bears the full title of the service and the motto "Fortitudo Mea Deus" - "God is my strength" - surrounding the entwined double-A cypher of Queen Alexandra.

QAIMNS(R) in silver; the badge is the reserve "R" surrounded by a garter bearing the full title.

(Right) The detachable sleeves, showing two of the four buttons used to secure each sleeve in place. Despite the simplicity of the new uniform the nurse's veil was still a high maintenance item, needing plenty of starch and ironing.

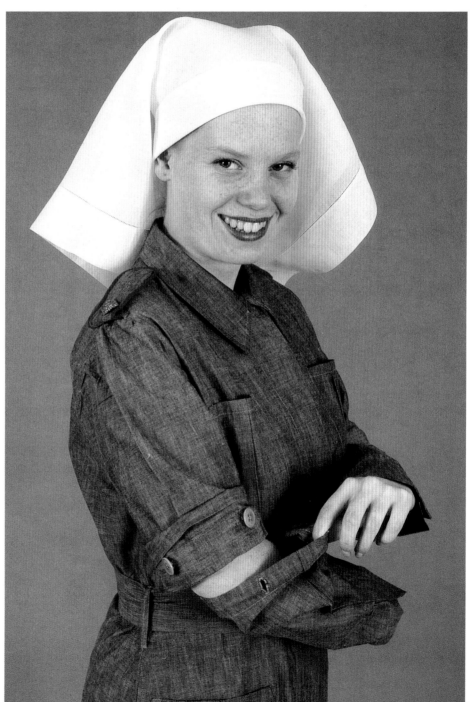

NURSE'S BATTLEDRESS

The nurse's immaculately starched and pressed ward dress was totally impractical for use under field conditions, as was proved by experience in North Africa. Consequently nursing sisters serving in the field were issued with battledress from 1942 - depending upon availability, either ATS pattern BD blouse and slacks or men's pattern BD blouse and trousers. In North-West Europe, 1944-45, it was common to see a mixture of both types being worn. As officers nurses officially wore rank badges on the epaulettes. Headwear was often dispensed with entirely, although the unlovely general service cap was standard issue and could be seen worn with the cap badge of the appropriate service.

Serving in close proximity to the front line and often well within range of enemy artillery and aircraft, nurses frequently had use for the steel helmet.

(Left) This nursing sister of the Queen Alexandra's Imperial Military Nursing Service (Reserve), serving in North- West Europe 1944-45, is kitted out entirely in men's pattern battledress uniform. The 1937 pattern trousers and blouse are of early manufacture, as shown by the lack of a cotton drill lining to the collar of the blouse. Men's clothing did not fit well, but was at least practical for duty in forward field locations. The emblem of British Troops in France is worn on both shoulders. The man's "Cap, GS" - an unflattering and generally unpopular headgear - is worn here with the QAIMNS(R) badge.

(Left) The white and maroon embroidered version of the QAIMNS shoulder title. Introduced late in the war, it was rarely seen on the battledress. An economy printed version also existed.

(Right) This Territorial Army Nursing Service Sister was photographed in France in the late summer of 1944. She is wearing an ATS battledress blouse with her service dress skirt, and a general service cap bearing the TANS badge, and carries an officer's private purchase mackintosh. The Army Captain accompanying her is wearing 1940 pattern trousers and 1937 pattern BD blouse; his sleeve patch is that of Second Army.

(Left) The badge of office of the QAIMNS(R), minted in sterling silver and worn on the front right corner of the tippet worn with ward dress.

NURSE'S ANTI-MOSQUITO UNIFORM

Many of the theatres of war in which Army nurses served - including parts of Italy in summer, as well as Africa and Asia - were prone to outbreaks of mosquito-borne malaria, which defied all the costly and time-consuming attempts made to eradicate it. In some regions it was sufficient protection at dusk - when the mosquitoes typically swarmed to feed - to button all clothing, roll down shirt sleeves and apply insect repellent to the face and hands. In other areas the risk of infection was so great that it was felt necessary to cover all exposed flesh, and special mosquito hoods and gloves were issued.

(Left) "Shirt, Mosquito, Nursing Officers." This shirt was similar in style to the bush jacket, but made of heavy cotton drill material. It could be fastened to the neck, and tightened at the wrist by a button and tab closure. For normal wear during periods when mosquitos were inactive the sleeves could be detached just above the elbow for better ventilation and comfort. It is worn here with anti-mosquito slacks and button-up spats. Mosquitos were allegedly unable to penetrate the fabric used for all these items.

(Below) "Spats, Mosquito, Nursing Officers." These were secured at the side by seven buttons, and a leather strap passed beneath the instep of the shoe to prevent them riding up over the ankle.

(**Above**) Full mosquito protection - the hood, worn here with the bush hat, anti-mosquito gloves, and the individual insecticide sprayer (DDT) shown in its box of three units.

THE WOMEN'S AUXILIARY AIR FORCE

Although the WAAF was officially formed in June 1939, by that date some 2,000 women in 48 companies of ATS volunteers produced by the 1938 recruiting drive had already been attached to the RAF, wearing khaki uniforms with distinguishing insignia. These companies were transferred as the nucleus of the Women's Auxiliary Air Force.

Initially there were only five trades for which WAAFs could train after completing their two weeks' basic training; but under the pressure of total war their role would soon expand enormously. During the desperate summer of 1940 the WAAFs came into their own, and two images of their service became immortalised in the public imagination: girls scarcely out of their teens gathered around the plotting tables of fighter sector stations, calmly putting on steel helmets over their headsets as the bombs of yet another heavy raid thundered towards them across the airfield; and the solitary WAAF concentrating intensely on the peaks and troughs of her primitive screen in one of the vital, and equally exposed, Chain Home radar stations.

A more physically arduous and equally important contribution to the air defences were the barrage balloons, manned and maintained by highly trained teams of WAAFs. Often in open, wind-swept locations, the women would winch aloft these lumbering giants to protect airfields and factories from low-flying raiders.

When the RAF turned to the attack, WAAF auxiliaries fulfilled countless tasks in immediate support of the aircrew. Reconnaisance photos were scrutinised by WAAF interpretation experts; WAAF storekeepers issued flying clothing and parachutes (which had been packed by WAAFs); WAAFs manned every kind of plotting and communications equipment during operations; and when the weary crews landed, WAAF MT drivers delivered them to the debriefing room, where WAAF officers would often interview them, before they gratefully slouched off to the mess for the coveted egg-and-bacon aircrew breakfast - cooked by WAAFs.

By late 1943 some 182,000 WAAFs were serving world-wide in 22 officer branches and 75 trades; they represented 16 per cent of the RAF's total strength, and 22 per cent of Home Command. It is difficult to adequately describe their contribution to final victory in the air. Their role can now be seen as indispensable to the intricate structure of the wartime air force, and extended far beyond mere "standing in" for their male comrades.

AIRCRAFTWOMAN'S SERVICE DRESS

The WAAF service dress - authorised in March 1939, though not available in quantity for some time - was inspired both by that of its parent service the ATS, and by the RAF airman's service dress uniform. Apart from the RAF blue colour the main distinctive features of the WAAF SD were the waist belt, and the black peak to the cap, both doubtless copied from the male airman's uniform, which in 1939 included a stiff-peaked SD cap. Unlike that of the ATS, the WAAF SD saw only minor subsequent design changes during the wartime years.

(Left) WAAF Aircraftwoman, 1942. The Royal Air Force blue uniform, with its pleated breast pockets, large tunic skirt pockets and integral waist belt, was made of a barathea cloth of finer quality than the rough serge of the men's SD. The two-gore skirt fastens on the left side with snap fasteners and a single button on the waistband, which is reinforced with petersham fabric. This WAAF has qualified as a Wireless Operator, as shown by the trade badge of lightning bolts in a clenched fist on her right sleeve.

(Below) The printed version of the RAF albatross badge, worn by male and female O/Rs at the top of each sleeve, with the albatross facing to the rear; and a woven "A" title denoting volunteer auxiliary status. After 1941 the "A" was less often seen, as recruits were more often conscripts than volunteers.

(Bottom) Detail of the label in the WAAF service dress tunic, showing its official designation - "Jacket, Serge, WAAF".

WEEKS
JACKET SERGE W.A.A.F.
Size No. 16
Height - 5 ft. 7 ins. to 5 ft. 8 ins.
Bust - 40 to 41 ins.
Waist - 32 to 33 ins.
JOSEPH MAY & SONS (LEEDS) LTD.
MAENSON HOUSE, LEEDS.
292/C/697N (Con 16D)
January, 1942

(Left) The WAAF cap took its basic design from that of the ATS. It has a black patent leather chinstrap and peak, the underside of the latter in green leatherette. The sides are internally reinforced. The standard RAF O/R's brass cap badge is worn on a band of black open-weave fabric.

(Right) Cap label showing size 7, RAF stores number, and year of manufacture; these details were often marked in white paint.

(Left) The WAAF service shoe, made of black dimpled leather with five pairs of lace eyelets. The distinctive feature is the "apron front," which both adds style and allows for the use of smaller sections of leather in the manufacture.

71

WAAF OTHER RANKS' GREATCOAT

It took over a year of war service for the Air Ministry to recognise the need for a purpose-made greatcoat for auxiliaries of the WAAF. The decision was undoubtedly spurred by the King's comments after having seen WAAFs shivering on parade dressed in flimsy raincoats while the RAF officers present were wearing greatcoats. Prior to the greatcoat's introduction in November 1940 the WAAFs had to make do with an improvised arrangement of commercial raincoats and overcoats.

This was in keeping with the experiences of the other women's services, and was partly due to the unexpected expansion of women's roles within the military: what need (it had doubtless been asked) had the office-bound clerk or kitchen chef of 1939 for a wool overcoat? This philosophy was soon proved short-sighted by bitter experience of many a wind-swept airfield and draughty hangar in the winter of 1939/40.

(Far left) Straight out of the QM's stores, this auxiliary is wearing her newly issued greatcoat, yet to have its regulation albatross badge sewn to the top of each sleeve. At a cursory glance it is not dissimilar to the airman's coat, but on closer inspection it is almost identical to the ATS greatcoat that was to be introduced in 1941 - though it differs in lacking epaulettes, there being no requirement for the wearing of titles. Internally it is fully lined in white cotton twill fabric.

(Below left) The early war raincoat, seen here being worn by a WAAF Corporal drummer in November 1939.

(Right) With the WAAF greatcoat buttoned to the neck, the "lancer"-style lines can be appreciated. It is fastened on the men's side with a double row of five RAF buttons - the airman's version had only four pairs.

(Below) Photographed in November 1940, members of the WAAF wearing their newly issued greatcoats. Typically, respirator haversacks are slung over their right shoulders.

WAAF 'SUIT, WORKING, SERGE'

The service dress uniform was considered unsuitable for many tasks on which WAAFs were employed; trousers were necessary for WAAFs working on balloon sites and for tradeswomen such as fitters and mechanics. During the early part of the war a variety of makeshift workwear had been issued; and it was not until early 1941 that the first female version of the male "Suit, Aircrew" (called "War Service Dress" from 1943) was issued - a Royal Air Force copy of the 1937 pattern Army battledress uniform. The WAAF version was designated "Suit, Working, Serge, WAAF", and its blouse closely followed the design of the male uniform, with a fly front and concealed buttons to the three-point flaps of the pleated breast pockets.

It was issued with slacks of a matching material. These were full cut, with a flap front secured by a row of three buttons on each side; a single internal pocket was placed on the right side; and two buttons on the rear of the slacks and one at the front secured them to matching buttonholes in the waistband of the blouse. A black beret, unique to the WAAF, was worn with the work suit on balloon sites and while employed on other duties for which the service dress cap was unsuitable. Most unusually for the British services, the beret was worn pulled down at the back of the head with the badge placed centrally at the front.

(Left) The "Suit, Working, Serge, WAAF" worn here by a Flight Mechanic (Aircraft), one of the many trades previously the preserve of male personnel in which WAAFs served with distinction. The blouse of the blue serge work uniform is worn here, unusually, with the albatross sleeve badges. The matching serge slacks, the black working beret and rubber boots complete the outfit.

(Below) Detail of the interior label in this 1943 blouse, manufactured by L.Harris Ltd.

SUITS, WORKING SERGE
WAAF
BLOUSES
Size No. 5
Height   5ft 7in—5ft 8in
Bust   34in—37in
Waist   26in—29in
L. HARRIS LTD.
August 1942

(Left) WAAF black rubber boots. Always in short supply due to the wartime shortage of rubber after the loss of Malaya, these were only issued when weather conditions made them absolutely necessary, and were re-soled rather than replaced.

(Above) The black beret, an item of RAF issue unique to the WAAFs, and used by those employed on dirty tasks.

(Below) A WAAF mechanic, wearing the black beret and RAF blue battledress-style work suit, undertakes salvage work on a Rolls Royce Merlin engine.

UTILITY PATTERN WORKING SUIT

A utility version of the working suit blouse was later produced with the usual aim of reducing cost in time and materials. Again, the simplifications were less radical than those made to the Army's battledress. The fly front was deleted and all the buttons were exposed, metal buttons being replaced by black plastic; and the buckle on the belt section fastening at the right front of the waist was replaced by an economy prongless pattern. However, the three-point pocket flaps typical of the RAF blouse was retained, as were the pocket pleats.

By the end of the war it was common to see the working blouse being worn with the service dress skirt, a mixing of uniform which had previously been considered unthinkable.

(Left & right) This WAAF medical orderly is dressed in the "Suit, Working, Serge, WAAF" with the utility pattern of blouse. She is carrying a first aid kit in an RAF blue-grey 1937 pattern small pack. In the close-up at right, note on this example the faced collar with the hook-and-eye removed; also the winged caduceus emblems worn on each collar point by members of the RAF medical services.

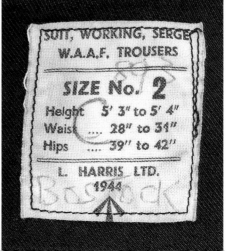

(Above right) WAAF ankle boots, as worn with working dress but not with service dress. Made of black pebble-grained leather, they have toecaps and eight pairs of eyelets.

(Left) The label on the utility version of the blouse. Note that no pattern distinction is made between this and the earlier design.

(Right) A WAAF Corporal medical orderly, photographed while tending Canadian wounded prior to an evacuation flight in a C-47 from an airstrip in the Normandy beachhead, summer 1944. When undertaking duties involving flying, WAAFs would be issued a loan of men's flying clothing including Irvin jacket, flying boots and "Mae West".

(Left) The label on the slacks for the WAAF "Suit, Working, Serge", in this case manufactured in 1944.

WAAF OFFICER'S SERVICE DRESS

The WAAF officer's service dress closely followed the design of that worn by Royal Air Force officers, but cut to female form. The tunic had pleated breast pockets with three-point flaps, and large external "bellows" skirt pockets with rectangular flaps; fastening to the male side, it had an integral cloth belt with a brass two-prong buckle, and all buttons were brass or gilt RAF pattern. Rank lace at the cuffs was also of the male pattern - varying numbers and widths of light blue lace on black backing - but with WAAF rank designations (see below). While WAAF auxiliaries wore a cloth "A" at the shoulder, officers wore a gilt metal "A" on both lapels of the tunic to signify their status. After December 1941 its use declined among officers and airwomen alike, as the bulk of new recruits were conscripts.

Shirts and stockings were generally of superior quality to those issued to airwomen, being privately purchased; officers' shirts were of a pale powder blue rather than the blue-grey issue type (although it was not uncommon for airwomen, too, to wear privately purchased shirts and stockings).

Work clothing was not initially issued to WAAF officers, whose duties were envisaged as being entirely supervisory. There were exceptions, however, and both WAAF and PMRAFNS officers wore working dress when conditions made it necessary. For WAAF officers the airwoman's battledress-style blouse was modified by the addition of epaulettes, at the base of which strips of rank lace were displayed.

WAAF rank structure 1939-45:

WAAF rank	RAF equivalent
Commandant in Chief	Air Marshal
Air Chief Commandant	Air Vice Marshal
Air Commandant	Air Commodore
Group Officer	Group Captain
Wing Officer	Wing Commander
Squadron Officer	Squadron Leader
Flight Officer	Flight Lieutenant
Section Officer	Flying Officer
Assistant Section Officer	Pilot Officer

(**Left**) This Squadron Officer wears the WAAF officer's service dress privately tailored in a fine blue-grey barathea. Note the light blue on black rank lace on the sleeves, here the one narrow between two broad stripes shared with the RAF rank of Squadron Leader.

(Right) Note details of the tunic, the cap, and the powder blue shirt worn by WAAF officers. The officers' pattern of cap had a distinctive three-section crown - note V-seams at the front - and a cloth-covered stitched peak.

(Below) The auxiliary "A" worn by volunteer WAAF officers on service dress lapels, and also above the rank lace on the shoulder boards of the greatcoat.

(Left) The badge worn by both RAF and WAAF officers on the service dress cap: a gilt albatross above a bullion wire wreath, all surmounted by the King's crown in natural colours.

79

WAAF LEATHER JERKIN

The leather jerkin issued to members of the WAAF was identical to that used by the ATS. It was made of heavy brown leather, and secured at the front by four large plastic buttons positioned on the left side of the jerkin. The internal lining was of a khaki serge blanket material. The only feature distinguishing the WAAF jerkin from the ATS issue is the label identifying it as such.

This "Jerkin, Leather, WAAF" was issued as an item of cold weather clothing for wear with working dress. It was not worn with service dress, with which the greatcoat was used.

(Left) The WAAF leather jerkin, worn here with the working dress by an MT driver. The marks of wear on the left skirt of the jerkin were typical of drivers, and were caused by abrasion from the gearstick, handbrake, or battery box, depending on the vehicle driven.

(Below) Detail of the label and khaki lining of a 1944-made WAAF jerkin.

WAAF SHIRT

The issue shirt was made from a light blue-grey cotton fabric. It had a full button front secured on the left (female) side, buttoned cuffs, and a small open-top patch pocket on the left breast. The shirt was cut for the female figure, having pleats at the narrow shoulder. WAAF auxiliaries were issued with three shirts, each having two detachable collars, which were secured to the shirt neckband centrally at front and rear by metal or plastic studs.

(Left) The WAAF shirt worn with the black tie and serge work slacks. Of note are the button arrangement and pleating on the slacks, and the single slash pocket on the right.

(Below left) RAF issue kitbag, the handle lockable with a padlock, named to a member of the WAAF.

(Below) Detail of the shirt showing the shoulder pleats, single patch pocket, and stiff detachable collar. This example has had the cuff button removed and a second hand-stitched buttonhole added so that cufflinks may be worn - an unofficial attempt to give a little feminine flair to government property.

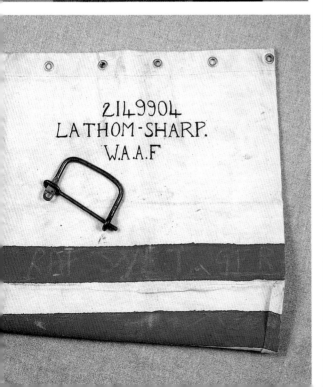

WAAF OVERALLS & WORK-WEAR

Not long after the WAAF's inception in 1939 it became apparent that for anything other than clerical duties the service dress was an unsuitable working uniform. One of the items issued to fill the need for a working suit was a one-piece fly-fronted combination overall made of dark blue heavy duty cotton fabric. This had a single open-top patch pocket on the left breast; side openings in the leg allowed access to any garment worn beneath, and a half-belt at the rear waist allowed some adjustment. Early overalls had a blue trim to the collar.

WAAFs were also issued a blue working wrap-over identical in style to that issued to the ATS in tan and green fabrics - see pages 50-51. (WAAF cooks had an ATS style white wrap-over; and special wooden-soled leather clogs for kitchen wear.)

The dark blue wrap-over working dress was later replaced, like its ATS counterpart, by a smarter "frock" pattern, with a central half-length closure fastened by six removable black plastic buttons, buttoned cuffs, a two-button half-belt at the rear waist, and two open-top patch pockets on the front of the hips.

(**Left**) A WAAF parachute packer inspects a deployed parachute to assess its condition for re-use or salvage. The type of dished brass button used on the combination overall is visible on the cuff. The service dress shirt and tie are worn beneath the overall. These WAAF rubber boots were made by Dunlop in 1944.

(Left) Close-up of the WAAF working overall, showing the patch pocket, and the Air Ministry's white stamped "crowned AM" marking visible on the inside of the collar. Repeated polishing has reduced much of the detail on the badge worn on this WAAF's cap; some "old hands" would polish all raised detail from the badge, leaving only a smooth outline of the emblem.

(Below left) Detail from a photo of a group of WAAF balloon repairers under instruction, some wearing overalls and some the early blue wrap-over. In the turned-back collars of some of these early-manufacture overalls (seated figures) a lighter blue trim can be seen. (Imperial War Museum)

(Below) "Clogs, WAAF", issued to cooks. These side-lacing clogs have a black leather upper nailed to a wooden sole, with leather reinforcing/anti- slip patches.

(Bottom) The second pattern WAAF working dress, this example dated 1941; note front button, seam and pocket details. This frock-cut working dress was worn either on its own or over the shirt and skirt or slacks.

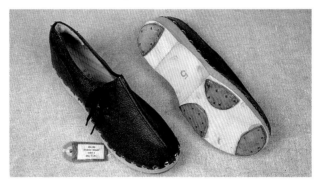

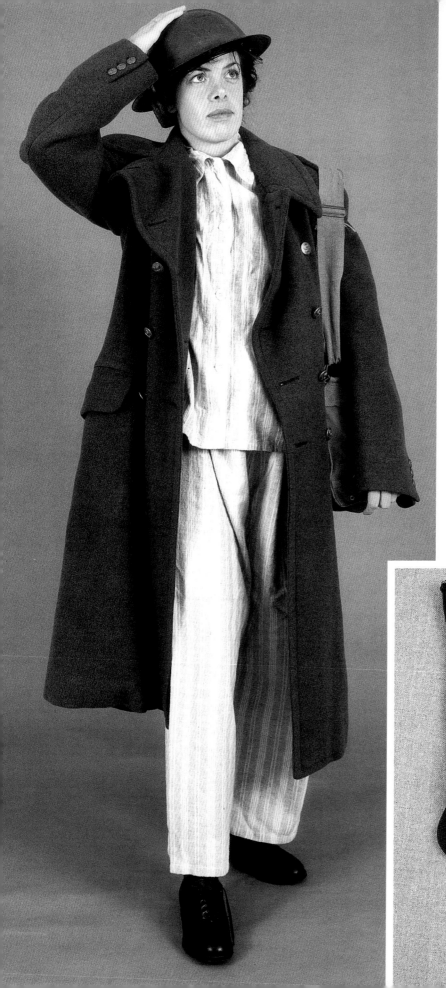

WAAF OFFICER'S GREATCOAT

(Left) "AIR RAID!" - this WAAF officer has reacted quickly to the warning siren, pausing only to grab her helmet, respirator and greatcoat before heading for the cold, damp shelter - where she may spend hours before the "All Clear" sounds, and where she will appreciate the warmth of the wool melton greatcoat. It is of a similar design to the airwoman's coat but with the addition of three ornamental buttons at each cuff, a full waist belt, and shoulder boards bearing rank lace and the gilt auxiliary officer's "A" device.

(Below) 1944-dated RAF issue socks, with a WAAF's name and W-prefix serial number marked on a cotton label stitched to the top of each. These are standard men's issue socks but in smaller women's size.

WOMEN'S PYJAMAS

(Left) Winceyette pyjamas issued to all three women's services conformed to the same standard design. The fabric was both warm and comfortable, and laundered well. It did not meet the expectations of many of the girls, however, who preferred to provide their own nightwear.

The blue and white striped pattern was also used on men's pyjamas, which on close inspection differed subtly. The woman's pyjama jacket fastened on the left side by four white plastic buttons. The pyjama trousers had no fly front, and were secured instead at a small expansion vent on the left hip by a tie string.

(Below) The ink-stamped date, size and manufacturer's marking on the pyjama jacket. Both parts of the suit illustrated also bear a WAAF's name and W-prefix serial number.

WAAF KD UNIFORM

From 1940 WAAF personnel had been posted overseas; but it was not until 1944 that such substantial numbers were serving in the hot climates of southern Europe, the Middle East and India that the issue of a purpose-made WAAF khaki drill uniform was felt necessary.

This issue consisted of a long-sleeved shirt, a bush jacket, slacks, a skirt, and khaki stockings. These were worn with the tie, shoes, and cap from the blue home service uniform. No specialised tropical headgear was issued, although from early 1944 WAAFs were authorised to wear the RAF field service cap, normally with black plastic buttons and badge.

The bush jacket was officially worn with the shirt and tie, skirt and lisle stockings, but this combination predictably proved too hot for comfort, and in practice the jacket was normally worn without a shirt and tie, and with short socks in preference to the stockings.

(Left) "Skirt, KD, WAAF" and "Jacket, Bush, WAAF", worn with khaki lisle stockings, black WAAF shoes and service dress cap. The bush jacket was issued with long sleeves, but it was common to see it re-tailored to a short-sleeve design for extra comfort. Wartime photographs show a good deal of latitude in uniform practice; an off-duty group might include the tropical shirt with or without the tie, the bush jacket with rolled or shortened sleeves, and sandals worn with ankle socks.

(Below) The label on a 1944-made khaki drill WAAF bush jacket. Note that this is not made from the open-weave Aertex material found in the ATS equivalent (see page 56).

(Above) Details of the bush jacket: two pleated breast pockets, and two patch pockets on the skirt; the belt (not stitched to the jacket) with a black metal two-prong buckle; and buttons of black plastic, bearing the RAF crown-over-albatross motif.

(Right) The WAAF tropical shirt, worn here with KD slacks and the RAF field service cap. The sidecap was standard issue to WAAFs in tropical theatres from early 1944. The slacks were worn in the cool of the evenings, or by those whose duties made the skirt unsuitable.

WAAF OFFICER'S BAZAAR KD

As with service dress, the WAAF officers' khaki drill uniform was styled on that authorised for RAF officers. In basic form it was a direct copy of the service dress uniform but manufactured in light khaki coloured cotton drill fabric. The main additions were pointed false cuffs on the jacket sleeves, and a box pleat in the KD skirt. Like the junior ranks, officers in the tropics wore khaki stockings instead of the home service blue type.

The regulation headgear was the tropical service pith helmet with a rectangular flash in the RAF colours displayed on the puggree at the side. However, the service dress cap was widely worn in preference to this bulky and somewhat unflattering headgear. Although airwomen had been authorised the field service cap for wear in the tropics in place of the SD cap from early 1944, this concession was not officially extended to WAAF officers. It was nevertheless a popular headgear with all ranks.

(**Left**) This WAAF Flight Officer, stationed somewhere in the Middle East in 1944, has purchased her own KD bush jacket - specifying non-regulation short sleeves - from a tailor in the local Arab bazaar. The purchase of locally produced uniform items was common among all the services; they were generally expertly tailored and inexpensive. The jacket is worn here without a shirt or tie, and with regulation KD slacks. (The combination of short sleeves and slacks is stylish and comfortable, while frustrating the official intention of covering the body as thoroughly as possible against mosquito bites.) For a sight-seeing trip she is carrying her "Box Brownie" camera in its case; and has acquired a Coke, doubtless courtesy of Our Gallant Allies.

(Right) The Royal Air Force officers' field service cap, made of a fine blue-grey wool barathea, and displaying its distinctive two-part gilt crown and albatross badge.

(Left) The various patterns of sun helmets issued in the tropics were generically known as "solar topees", from the Hindustani for "hat". This "Wolseley" pattern, dating from the days of Kitchener at Omdurman, was particularly unwieldy, and unpopular in the 1940s. Note the WAAF Flight Officer's rank lace worn on KD epaulette slides.

PMRAFNS SERVICE DRESS

The RAF Nursing Service had existed since the earliest days of the Royal Air Force, being formed in June 1918; however, it was not until 1923 that the title Princess Mary's Royal Air Force Nursing Service was adopted. The PMRAFNS officially acquired armed forces status in 1941; however, the single rank stripes of the different "appointments" (light blue on maroon for Matrons and Senior Sisters, light on dark blue for Sisters) continued to be worn until March 1943. In that month Air Ministry Order 196 announced that henceforward the "PMs" would wear the same light blue and black lace rank insignia as the RAF and WAAF while retaining their own nursing titles. Comparative ranks were:

PMRAFNS	RAF equivalent
Matron-in-Chief	Air Commodore
Principal Matron	Wing Commander
Matron	Squadron Leader
Senior Sister	Flight Lieutenant
Sister	Flying Officer
Staff Nurse (until 1/4/1941)	Pilot Officer

(Left) This PMRAFNS Sister is wearing the blue-grey barathea summer service dress, with its distinctive "Norfolk"-cut jacket and long skirt. The jacket has a broad pleat running down both sides of the front and back from hem to hem. The jacket front is secured by three gilt RAF buttons, with a cloth waist belt fastened by two more. Post-March 1943 rank lace is worn at the cuffs. The skirt has two smaller pleats, in line with the jacket pleats but running only down the front. The skirt is worn longer than was then fashionable, and falls to within ten inches of the ground. This uniform was worn with black shoes and stockings, white shirt and black tie.

Winter service dress was a blue-grey barathea coat-frock with long sleeves, stand collar, half-length front closure with 12 small gilt buttons, appointment/rank lace on the cuffs, and a matching tippet with gilt caduceus emblems in the front corners.

(Below) The label in the Norfolk jacket; Boyd Cooper were the main manufacturers for all the nursing services.

(Right) A 1943 publicity photograph showing a group of PMRAFNS sisters, all wearing summer service dress, with the two authorised hats (see details on page 92). The Sister standing at left wears the black "four-cornered" hat, the others the blue-grey storm cap. (Imperial War Museum)

Boyd-Cooper
LIMITED
12, Bruton Street,
London. W.1

(Right) Detail of the jacket, white shirt and black tie; the PMs' white shirt was unique within the RAF. Note the winged caduceus emblems worn on the jacket collar points.

(Below) The waist belt fastening; unadjustable, it is secured by two RAF buttons. This style of fastening is typical of nursing uniform of the period, also being used on many civil and military versions of the ward dress.

PMRAFNS WARD DRESS

General duties were carried out wearing the ward dress. Typical of nursing uniforms of the period, the white cotton dress had short sleeves, a half-length front closure secured by 14 buttons, a three-button waistbelt, and an open-top patch pocket positioned on each hip. Detachable shoulder boards displayed rank lace, on maroon backing for Matrons and Senior Sisters pre-March 1943. A plain tippet in RAF blue-grey, with the caduceus emblem on each point, was often worn with this uniform.

(Left) PMRAFNS nurse sterilising medical instruments; she wears white ward dress, with the head veil but without shoulder boards or tippet. Note details of the white dress, with rounded collar, 14 front buttons and a buttoned waist belt, and two patch pockets at the hips. (Imperial War Museum)

(Below left) Two PMs seen from a useful angle. At left, note the tippet, and the distinctive light blue PMRAFNS emblem on the rear point of the veil. The sister on the right is wearing an officer's greatcoat with rank lace on the shoulder boards; and the PMs' distinctive black hat, not dissimilar to the tricorn worn by WRNS officers and senior rates but with an "extra corner" at centre rear. (Imperial War Museum)

(Below right) Detail from a photo of a PM tending wounded in Belgium, January 1945. Although she wears field dress she retains the service dress storm cap rather than the blue-grey RAF beret authorised for field use. The storm cap is generally similar to the WAAF SD cap but has a small false peak/flap at the front. It is worn with the RAF officer's SD cap badge (as is the four-cornered hat in the photo below left). (Imperial War Museum)

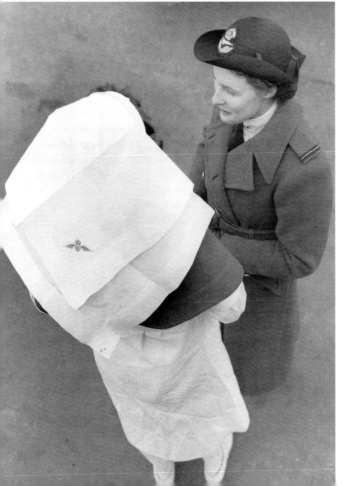

PMRAFNS FIELD UNIFORM

Like those of the other nursing services, the PMs' ward dress was unsuitable for use under field conditions. They therefore adopted the "Suit, Working, Serge" for field use; since all PMs held officer status it was necessary to have epaulettes added to the WAAF blouse to display rank lace. The white shirt and black tie were retained, but, unusually, PMs often wore their service dress skirt in preference to the slacks normally worn with the working suit blouse.

(Left & below) A PMRAFNS Sister serving near the front in NW Europe; at her feet is the large field first aid kit, and she holds a souvenir German helmet - perhaps a gift from a grateful wounded soldier evacuated through her forward airfield? She wears a steel helmet; the utility version of the WAAF "Suit, Working, Serge" blouse; and, as was common practice, the service dress skirt. The blouse has added officer's epaulettes and rank lace; and the sister has adopted the RAF practice of attaching a whistle to the collar fastening. In this case she does not have the caduceus collar emblems, but wears a red cross brassard.

(Detail) The crowned, winged caduceus emblem usually worn by all members of the RAF medical and nursing services.

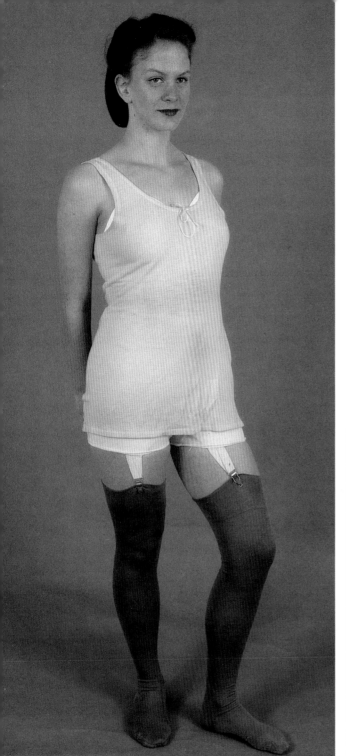

ISSUE UNDERWEAR

Upon enlistment women were issued all of the clothing and "necessaries" they required, including items such as underwear, toothbrushes, hairbrushes, etc., in addition to the military uniform and equipment. There was no requirement for any kit to be provided at the individual's own expense.

Issue of underwear was rationalised among the services, the same standard designs being adopted where possible. The items illustrated here for issue to a WAAF could just as well have been issued to an ATS auxiliary. WAAF items were frequently marked with the crowned AM of the Air Ministry, but this was not invariable, and many WAAF issue items are found with the War Department's broad arrow mark.

Compared to the elegant and very feminine lingerie available on the civilian market in the 1940s, the military issue was grimly unbecoming. A token effort had been made in the choice of pink as the standard colour for brassieres and suspender belts, but this was offset by their utilitarian design. A typical issue of underwear would include three pairs of stockings, two pairs of knickers, two pairs of wool panties, two vests, two long-line brassieres, and two suspender belts or corselets.

(Above) Warm and serviceable, but hardly flattering: this WAAF is wearing an issue wool vest, wool panties, WAAF blue-grey lisle stockings and pink suspender belt.

(Above right) The pink service issue suspender belt bearing an Air Ministry stock number, and WAAF lisle stockings dated 1942 and Air Ministry marked.

(Right) WAAF knickers and panties. On the left, RAF blue knickers (also issued in khaki for the ATS and dark blue for the WRNS), and on the right two variations of the wool panties, one bearing the crowned "AM" and dated 1941.

MISCELLANEOUS DOCUMENTS

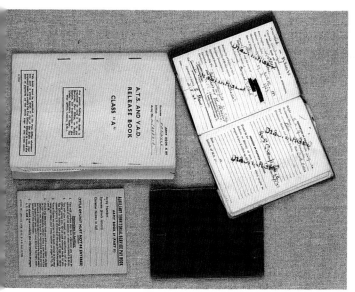

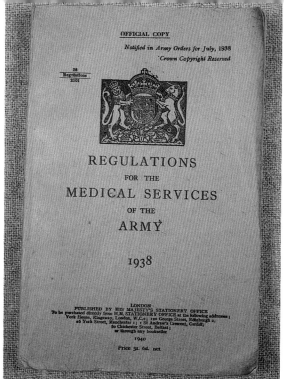

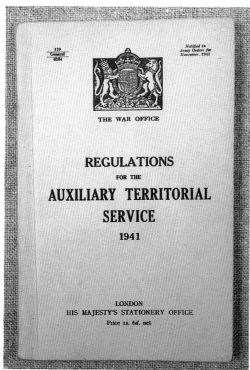

(Top left) ATS paybook Part I & Part II; ATS/VAD release book; and open ATS paybook with details of holder and "Discharged" stamps.

(Top right) Regulations for the Medical Services of the Army, 1938. This publication listed the stringent requirements for candidates wishing to enter the QAIMNS; as well as physical and mental fitness, general appearance was considered highly important.

(Centre left) Regulations for the Auxiliary Territorial Service - this supplemented King's Regulations, with additions specific to female service personnel.

(Centre right) Vehicle maintenance manuals, as issued to ATS mechanics. "For BFs" was a humorous booklet published by the Bedford Motor Co. and aimed at junior ranks; the other is an official 1942 WD publication covering basic vehicle maintenance.

(Left) Leave passes made out to WAAF Aircraftwoman McLachlan while serving at RAF Station Turnberry, Scotland, in 1945.